The Riots

Danielle Cadena Deulen

The Riots

THE UNIVERSITY OF GEORGIA PRESS

ATHENS & LONDON

Published by the University of Georgia Press

Athens, Georgia 30602

www.ugapress.org

© 2011 by Danielle Cadena Deulen

Designed by Walton Harris

Set in 10/15 Garamond Premier Pro

Printed and bound by Thomson-Shore

The paper in this book meets the guidelines for permanence
and durability of the Committee on Production Guidelines
for Book Longevity of the Council on Library Resources.

Printed in the United States of America

15   14   13   12   11   C   5   4   3   2   1

Library of Congress Cataloging-in-Publication Data

Deulen, Danielle Cadena.
The riots / Danielle Cadena Deulen.
      p.   cm.
ISBN-13: 978-0-8203-3883-5 (cloth : alk. paper)
ISBN-10: 0-8203-3883-4 (cloth : alk. paper)
I. Title.
PS3604.E84R56 2011
814'.6—dc22   2010049359

British Library Cataloging-in-Publication Data available

For my mother

Contents

The Riots

Still Life
with Flashing
Lights

Our limbs move us down the stairway. We've been sleeping. Our bodies are heavy and eyes sensitive to the early morning light, so we approach the scene in silence. Still, our mother presses her finger to her lips before we all descend the stairs, her broad face as tense as an electric wire. At the landing, the living room opens up to us—dark wood paneling walls, the couch with the autumn-colored ticking (orange and brown leaves curling in a matrix of yellow gold). At the farthest end of the room is a wall of dark, built-in shelves cluttered with books, none of which have been opened for years. To the right, two large windows are heavy eyed with half-drawn shades. Between the two windows, our front door is wide open, and our brother stands on the threshold—his brown eyes wide, biting the tips of his fingers. Opposite the door, against the wall, is a worn upright piano that's never been tuned, and beneath the piano stool is our father's unlaced boot, tongue lolling. All over the wood floor are splinters from the smashed coffee table. At the center of the room is our unconscious father, fully clothed, his limbs splayed out like those of a starfish. Police lights from the car outside flash through the window onto his still chest and face—his blue eyes shut behind their lids and his dark beard curling—

a frayed blanket. We're afraid he's dead but more afraid that he'll rouse, so we have to be careful as we step over his legs toward the door. We move so slowly it's as if we aren't moving at all. Figures in a painting. Our mother carries our youngest sister (thick arms around our mother's neck) and waits at the landing, gestures for us to go ahead. My sister Jasmine (her coiled honey hair) and I hold hands as we step through the room. Her small bust is like a finely made screen—blue and red lights flash across the smooth white of her forehead, her soft cheeks, her thin shoulders. Outside, just past my brother, a tall man in a blue uniform (hand placed lightly on his holstered gun) waves us toward our half-packed Chevy. We're going on another trip. Already I see how we'll return.

Theft

I wake hungry in the dry heat. Outside my window, beyond the dense black fever of the parking lot, sweetgrass marks the edge of the arroyo. Salt at the corners of my mouth. The sun glares in. My dreams were full of dark hallways, roads, strangers—red somewhere in each scene—always something leading me to a feast, then leading me away.

I dress, put on sandals, grab my messenger bag, and leave the apartment. No rain to soak down the arroyo, so dust rises around me as I walk through it. The other side opens to an empty lot of busted concrete, thigh-deep grass, and low patches of chamisa, that saltbush of rough yellow clouds. It leads to the ugly back of a grocery store.

A few days before, I'd stolen enough food for the week, but now it's all gone. When I started, I was careful to take only as much as I needed. But excess leads to excess. It's a kind of sickness to always feel lack—eats away at my mind.

I know the universe is not in debt to me. Still, I'm hungry. Just at the edge of the field, I stub my toe on a dull plate of concrete. When I bend down to assess the sting, I see the tiniest stream of blood bordering my nail. Dust and blood. In the thicket of chamisa, something scurries away.

"I'm not judging you," I say to my father on the phone, looking out of my window toward a stand of bare trees, "I'm just trying to understand what happened." He'd been released from jail a month before and still the facts I'd gathered about that night wouldn't cohere. I was hundreds of miles away when it happened and everyone who called had something heavy on their tongues.

"Did you steal something?"

"Do you think I would steal something?"

No, I thought, *that isn't in your repertoire.* He worked construction, his body a hard sculpture of healed wounds and muscle, and was proud of his work, of the way it had provided for him and for us. He would never do something as shameful, as vulgar, as stealing. I could imagine his chest swelling out when he said it, his weathered hands forming a fist.

"No."

"Yeah, that's the bitch of it. Anytime you break into someone's house it's called burglary. So now anyone who looks at my record will think I'm a thief. I'm no thief."

"I know."

"If anyone asks, you tell them that."

"Okay."

"I didn't steal anything. I just broke into her house."

They lived in Oregon. His fiancée was a tall, slender redhead and they fought as often as it rained. Since strife was the fabric of their love, he couldn't remember what they'd fought about the night before—the reason they called off the wedding, left screaming in different directions. Then she went out to the place they would sometimes go dancing, where she chose a different man, rubbed her body against him to the music in the dark. My father watched from a corner, swallowing gall and the amber burn of whiskey until he'd made up his mind to hurt her.

"To disrespect me like that after everything. She was going to be my wife, goddamnit, my fucking *wife*." He said that she saw him—flaunted it—kissed the man in front of him, and left with her hands in his pockets. My father left just after, drove to her building to watch her enter her apartment with the stranger. Her bedroom light flickering briefly on, then off. He decided to go in.

He'd been sleeping there for a year, knew which window would be slightly open, and drifted in like a cloud. He paused in the kitchen—countertops cluttered with dirty plates, and next to the cutting board, a knife. It wasn't so much that she'd hurt him (she had) or that she was touching another man (she was), but that she would dare to announce her physical volition, unchain her body from my father's desires, that enraged him most. It was not that the man was a thief, but that she'd given herself away. He picked up the knife, walked the few steps through her dim apartment to her bedroom, the door slightly ajar, and went in.

The other man jumped up when my father entered, stood over the bed with his hands out, half in readiness, half in supplication.

"The guy got up but didn't get close. He was afraid—it was dark, but I could sense it." She was afraid too, but stayed silent, pulled the covers up over her chest, waiting. My father sprang over, gripped her pale arm, wound her red hair around his fist, and put the knife to her throat. For a long while they were fixed in this frame—a trilogy of forms around a dark bed, all barely visible in the ghost-light from the window. Only the knife trembled.

꙳

My father hands me a tiny wolf whose name we don't yet know. She yelps and trembles against my chest. Just hours before, she was pulled from her mama's den and sold to my father. The owners of the farm trapped the she-wolf in a barbed wire kennel to get at her litter, and my father was there when they did it—watched her pace and scream and bare her teeth. "That bitch made devil sounds," he tells me and in the same breath asks if I can watch the cub a while. Caring for puppies is women's work. I say yes. Her heart stammers in my palm.

When my father shuts the door she flinches. Her whimper rolls into a cry, then a plaintive howl. I know that sound. She twists and pushes, so I look for a soft place to land her. She flops out of my arms onto my mattress and buries herself in my blankets. I hear her little paws trying to dig, so I gather the blankets around her, loose but close. She stops digging and begins to cry. "Oh, come on now, baby, I'm not that bad," I lift the covers to her stunned silver eyes. She wriggles deeper in the blankets, away from the lamplight, so I put her in the dark again, lie down beside the cotton den and wait.

She circles and circles herself until she finally lies down. I pull back the covers, slower this time, and she doesn't tense when she sees me. I lean my face into her face and she keeps her breath steady, little tongue stuck out. She stretches her front paws forward and looks around, glassy-eyed, yawns, lays her small, gray head on her small, gray paws. Her markings are lighter around her eyes and a sharp white line divides the center of her face from the top of her head to the tip of her snout. "My father's white," I tell her, "He thinks he can own anything." To show her I'm true, I lick the top of her head. In return, she licks my paw. She closes her eyes and I close my eyes. We both begin to dream.

✳

"Did I ever tell you that story, from the Campillo side?" my mother asks, her long, dark hair sweeping across her face, getting caught in the corner of her mouth. It's windy today, but warm. We're downtown, away from the empty lots that throw dust like a curse. We're walking the smooth streets that wind toward and away from St. Francis Cathedral.

"I think I've heard it before. Our great, great, however many *greats* grandmother was the most beautiful in her village and, when the Spaniards came, a Castilian nobleman saw her, fell in love, and made her his wife."

"Yes. She was cooking, squatting in the dust, and he rode over on his white horse and swooped her up from the ground, and they were in love."

"Just like that."

"Yes, just like that."

This is my mother's first time in Santa Fe and she wants to see all the things I usually avoid. She wants to go to the oldest buildings, hear about the conquests of the Spanish, then the Americans, how the city was burned and built, burned and built. Everything looks adobe even if it isn't—a city ordinance to maintain its mystique. It's a tourist town, and survives on romance—the nostalgia of itself. We walk past the Navajo and Pueblo artisans lined on Palace Avenue, their straight gazes and stiff blankets sprawling with turquoise. We walk in and out of the galleries that sell paintings of coyotes howling at huge, looming moons, and the stores that sell solid gold belt buckles. There is good art in Santa Fe, and real diversity, but this isn't where to find it.

Still, I'm content to walk beside my mother, who smiles a lot, and is as even as a plateau. As I child, I always knew the borders of her patience, and she was only stern with me when I crossed them. Otherwise, she was generous and affectionate, quick to encourage me toward any endeavor, even after my father left, when she was both dark and bright with pain. When she finds anything delightful, she squeezes my hand or loops her arm around mine, and her hair brushes its gardenia scent into my face.

"You know the story is probably a lie," I tell her. "I mean, if he was a conquistador, he probably raped her and called her his wife after."

"Why do you have to say that?" She says, frowning, "It's a nice story."

"But it's not a true story."

"Stories don't have to be true for you to like them."

"They do if we tell them like they're true. If we say, *This is how our family began.*"

"But you don't know. It could be true. There's no one left to ask. So, why not believe the more beautiful version? I like to think they were in love."

"Because of everything it implies. It's that racist bullshit that says the native people were somehow better off by the Spanish arriving. Otherwise, they would have been *cooking in the dirt*, worshiping *false idols*. That thing that says, *Even if we're all the same mixed blood, the lighter you are, the better.*"

By now my mother has made the slightest space between us and folds her arms across her chest, looks away.

"Maybe," she says, "but you can't know for sure."

She's right, of course: I can't. So I hush. We let the story walk beside us a while, saying nothing for itself. In a block or so we'll forget it. I'll point out the rose window in the cathedral and she'll touch my shoulder. Or I'll point out something small and beautiful—a silver bowl, a blown glass vase—that we can't afford to buy. Or one of us will say we're hungry, find a little place to eat, and we'll sit down together, perhaps drink a little tequila with sweet and sour, and we'll forget. We'll talk about the food, the dreams we've had lately, what else we want to see that day. We'll weigh in on the family gossip, vacillating between advice and sympathy. We'll let the food and the sense of communion rise in our faces like a kind of light. Then we'll walk back to the car, drive toward my small apartment, and wonder at the bright red and gold of the sun, how it seems to set into the dark roofs of the adobe casitas. We agree it is an Old West sunset—as beautiful as it is in the movies. We can almost see a man like my father riding alone with his shotgun into those unknowable hills.

Dark Mother, you are the prettiest—lantern in a land of ravines—your eyes like copper bells ringing from towers not yet torn down. All your life you have watched the horizon, anticipating—the sky a cornflower blue you crush in your mortar. The resin of fermented agave and your mother's tongue will be swallowed by a foreign alphabet. You don't yet know this.

You are sick of drought, the taste of dog meat. You are stubborn and pure as wild chamisa, tie your virgin-black hair like a crown on top of your head. You are sitting near a fire beneath a deep-rooted sumac when a man with skin as fair as clouds rides on his white horse over the hills toward you, and as if struck by lightning, you both fall in love.

He reaches down, draws you up from the earth, presses you to his chest for the rest of his life. You bear him many sons, paler and paler with each birth, until the last child is as pale as the crest of a wave. This is why the first born Campillo is always dark, like you, and the rest of the children are milk. This is what our family tells me.

But the story ripens like inedible fruit—as poisoned, bitter, and bruised as your face, your wrists, in the morning dusk of that first consummation. History tells us no one fell in love. There were only rites of rifles and disease—a rite of teeth in your soft-spiced shoulder. Throat gripped closed. The broken skin at the base of your thighs. Thumbs to eyes. A child swelling and swelling into silence or into a story you can't untell.

It was love, we say it again and again, until it becomes myth, so no longer a lie. Sumac retreats from the south-facing window. A white horse hangs in the sky.

Aperture

Optics. An opening, usually circular, that limits the quantity of light that can enter an optical instrument.

I have seen my brother's eyes very few times. Eye contact is always brief—he tries to escape it whenever possible. Watching is an act of great importance for him. Merely glancing at him is an offense. Looking at him intently could result in a tantrum. His tantrums are huge, vocal, physical attacks. He is the unstable element: eyes like Lithium. *Just look at it and it will explode.* Flashes of dark brown—flecks of gold—or is it the way the light shines off them? What I know I've stolen through the years.

In a yellowed photo of my brother taken a month after his birth, his pale face is blank, his pupils wide in the dim light. It's a close-up: just his face and shoulders. The dark afghan my mother made is wrapped around him loosely, fuzzes up around his chin. No one is holding him. He looks calm. A deeper perspective is impossible—the room blurs behind him. I think of the birth I wasn't alive to witness.

My mother is glistening and exhausted beneath the high ceiling of their living room. Strands of her long dark hair stick to her forehead and broad cheeks. She's delirious with pain. My father has a hand on her round stomach and a hand pressing open a medical book—he's sweating too, glancing between her face, the book, a clock chiming on the wall. It's been thirty-six hours, and still no baby boy. Thirty-six hours is too long. They know that much. Too late to find a midwife, too poor to pay for a hospital. She has to push harder. *I wanted my hands to be the first hands to hold all of you*, my father often told us, *I wanted you to know the hands that would protect you.*

When my mother finally contracted Micah from her body, he didn't make a sound. Slick with blood and membrane, his eyes stared around the room, but took in nothing. Our mother was too drained to lift him. My father wrapped him in blankets, and laid him on the bed between them. Micah didn't cry until she touched him.

Autism is marked by abnormal introversion and egocentricity. Autism is not a personality disorder. It is a developmental disorder with a spectrum of symptoms so varied as to be almost unique to each individual. Emotional expression varies. Verbal skill varies. If you've met one person with autism . . . you've met one person with autism. Not all autistic people are idiot savants. Not all autistic people are mentally retarded. No one knows what creates autism. No one can bring it to light. Not all lights can be adjusted. Not all lights can help you to see. If autism could create photographs, each one would be overexposed. A light strong enough to burn us to it. Pictures that needle the nerves.

My mother was pregnant when she met my father. She was early on, so neither of them knew it. Micah was the culmination of a two-year love between my mother and a man named Jamie. He was from a well-off Sacramento family, deep in law and politics. She worked behind the counter of a Dairy Queen, part-time while she studied at the university where they met. She still smiles when she speaks of Jamie—how it took her months to work up the nerve to speak to him. She sighs. She shakes her head. "I was crazy for him."

A month before she met my father, Jamie broke up with her—said they got along too well, not enough charisma together, she agreed with him too often, etc. She cried and cried and walked to and from her job at the Dairy Queen, where my father was becoming a regular. He said he liked the way she stirred the shakes and asked her out. They'd only been out a few times when she learned she was two months pregnant.

She told my father and he said, "Marry me."

"But it's not your baby."

"Marry me anyway."

But then Jamie came back into the scene. He said he didn't love her but he didn't want an illegitimate child coming back to haunt his future political career. My mother told him she would marry my father and Jamie changed his mind. Wanted her, wanted to fight my father.

It's the famous scene with the two men in the yard with their fists clenched like fleshy bouquets, my mother waiting in the open air, her hands across the slight swell of her belly.

My father says, "You're going fight me, rich boy? Think for a minute. How many fights have you been in? How many fights do you think I've been in?" I imagine my father had just arrived home from work—his tanned arms and shoulders tense beneath a swath of dirt. Jamie thought better of it and sunk into silence, turned away.

The marriage took place in a park—everyone in embroidered muslin with flower wreaths in their hair. In the wedding slides there is a picture: my mother in a sun spot, looking down at her belly, swollen like a moon over her bare feet—she holds my father's hand. He is in a shadow, his wild hair and eyes, as dark as curling leaves. He is looking just out of the frame, to something disconcerting in the distance.

Turn away. It's easy to turn away. It's much easier than looking directly. Don't look here. *Don't look at me*. My brother walks quickly with his head down, arms stiff at his side, moving back and forth mechanically.

Or he paces. He paces around the room sometimes and is unable to stop.
Unable to stop making repetitive motions and sounds, fragments of sentences, noises that have no connection to the context (screech, yelp, pop, clap). He hits himself in the head. *Stupid. Retard.* When strangers come, he keeps to the corners, twitching and grinning wide, but unable to approach. Afraid to approach. The strangers I mean. Are afraid to approach. They don't know what he'll do. They don't know what to say. I don't know what to do. I don't know what to say. It's embarrassing. I'm embarrassed for him, for them, for myself. A brave stranger holds out his hand and walks toward Micah slowly, speaking evenly, as if Micah were a stray dog let in to the house. My father says, amused, "Say hi, Micah." Micah grins like a stray dog let into the house. I turn away. It's easier to turn away.

*

I was born. A year later, Mount St. Helens erupted. Ash covered my parents' land in Ryderwood, Washington, and made it barren. They moved to the city. My father got a job working construction. Days they argued about the money they didn't have, and nights he stayed out later and later. My sister Jasmine was born. Then Mileah.

We couldn't survive on his paychecks. Our mother got a waitress job working nights at Pancake Corner, hoping she'd make enough to help. She'd come in late and kiss our elbows to check if we were sleeping. There was no way to tell her what was happening when she was gone.

My father came home each day from the job site, red eyed and slow, landed heavily on our dying sofa, untied his construction boots one notch at a time. We were allowed to play in the yard if it wasn't raining, and to watch TV if it was. Then he'd drink and keep drinking—cracking open can after can of cheap beer. If we were quiet enough, he'd pass out in the shifting blue light of the television screen and we could brush our teeth, tiptoe to bed, and lie awake, waiting for our mother to come home. We were safe when our mother got home.

Sometimes I pretended to sleep when she came into my room. Sometimes I sat up to say hi, and she'd shush me back down.

"How was your night?"

"Good," I'd say. How I could tell her what was happening?

What I mean to say is my father beat him. Almost every day. It became ritual: my brother would begin his questions, or rock, or mumble, or laugh to himself, which would instigate my father. I always come back to this, the undertones of fault: *Micah instigates. He gets what he asked for.* It's the voice of my father explaining himself again. Micah is downstairs in his room, shaking. Mom is at work, so can't wedge herself between them like she does when she's home. It gets out of hand. It always gets out of hand. And then my father comes to find us girls to explain that he loves us all. *But your brother has problems. He makes things hard—you know how hard he makes everything. And I'm so tired, I just don't have the patience. And then he just won't stop, you know? I don't mean it to get out of hand, but he keeps at me . . . and besides, who knows how much he remembers—understands?*

My father is lovely when he's calm. So strong and lovely. He lifts the air to make us believe. This is the voice of the magician, who could wave his hand and be kind or cruel, who could carry us on his back, or bare his teeth, or make us completely disappear.

I've heard the story so many times it becomes myth. My brother is not my brother, but the archetype of brothers. We heard of him in a bedtime story. We keep him shut. Light never falls on him. I can pace around the violence of the room, the small opening of my memory, create a story that I can walk away from: The Myth of the Boy Raised by Wolves. The Myth of the Coward. The story in which I am transformed to a tree. *Who knows how much he remembers—understands?* My roots digging down into silence.

Cowardice is marked by ignoble fear in the face of danger or pain. Autistic people have an atypical sense of and response to fear. My brother is terrified if approached unannounced, but might walk into interstate traffic if no one redirects him. Autism is not caused by bad parenting. It is thought to be the result of abnormal brain development, particularly in the cerebellum and the limbic system. Abnormal brain development can be caused by most anything, and often doesn't result in autism. Danger and pain can be caused by most anything, and often don't result in cowardice. Cowardice is an adjustable opening in one's psyche that limits the amount of light that can enter.

*

I don't remember how it started, if there was anything to start it. My father came home red eyed and wired, ready for a fight. Micah said something, did something. I don't know. I can't remember. I grabbed Jasmine and Mileah and ran up the stairs with them to my room—stayed there holding their heads to my shoulders, covering their ears so they couldn't hear. I heard everything, but couldn't make a complete scene of it: clips of violence without context: wailing, falling, scraping, yelling, something wooden against the wall. My brother against the wall. They moved around the house in a circle—my father approaching, my brother retreating, until they reached my brother's room, just below mine, where the worst of it rose up through the floorboards—fist to rib to back to thigh, the breath knocked out of him and knocked out of him, a choking sound, a dense thud.

Then it stopped, suddenly, like a sharp exhale. I heard my father's boots across the living room, out the front door, the door slamming shut behind him. I let my hands drop to my sides. Jasmine and Mileah slumped against each other, whimpering. I pulled a blanket from my bed to cover them, then edged my way carefully down the stairs, the lit hallway, to Micah's room. When I opened his door, a sliver of light pointed across the dark to his pale form crouched in the corner—head between his knees, one arm over his neck, the other reaching up, flat palm trembling.

I stood there a while behind the light without telling him it was me—without giving him reason to uncoil. I knew beneath his lids his eyes were swollen from crying, and I did nothing. The light opened him to me—a narrow slit adjusting in my psyche—and I was a silhouette, watching his skinny arm raised toward my shadow.

"It's just me," I said, finally. When he heard my voice he let his arms down, slowly. "I'm just here to see if you're okay." He dropped his arms down completely then looked up, glassy-eyed, to a spot above my head—the light? Does he see me at all? *Who knows how much he remembers—understands?*

"Yeah," he said finally.

"Yeah?"

"Yeah, I'm fine now. I'm fine." I walked into the unlit room, shut the door behind me, and sat down on the edge of the bed. He got up from the corner and sat next to me. The room was opaque at first, but slowly my eyes adjusted so that I could see him. A light shone in from somewhere, glossing his face in silver. I can't remember how long we sat there in silence.

"I'm sorry," I said, finally.

"Why are you sorry? You didn't do anything."

But I didn't have an answer.

I stood in Ockley Green Middle School's field—a short expanse of matted-down grass and dirt patches hemmed in by a chain-link fence that separated the milling students from the traffic of Interstate Avenue. Keisha's thick form, made thicker by a black down parka, walked briskly out of the heavy metal doors and across the field to find me. She was caramel colored and lovely, her hair always slicked back into a spiky black ponytail, her eyes a disarming hazel.

"Micah's your brother, right?" Whenever she brought up my brother, she always began this way, as if at any moment I would reveal that all along I'd been lying. Her suspicions were valid. Until a few months ago, she didn't even know I had a brother. I didn't sit with him at lunch, or even talk to him in the hallways. If I happened to pass him, I'd wave hello and he'd wave back, speeding along in his brisk, twitching walk, his permanent grin—but nobody paid attention in the hallways, so nobody knew. I'd only mentioned he was my brother a few months ago because she and I were talking to Giovanni and Alfonzo—two boys from our class—when they started (perhaps to impress us?) making fun of *the retard* by the fence. Micah paced back and forth beneath a huge Douglas fir, talking to himself, sometimes laughing, smashing his hands over his mouth. It made me angry.

"Actually, that's not cool," I started, but the guys kept laughing.

"What? Like he's your best friend or something?" Alfonzo rolled his face near mine.

"Awww, that's sweet! You love him!" Gio said, placing his hands over his heart as if swooning.

"Yeah, actually, I do," I said, deadpan.

"You sweat that retard boy?!" Keisha's exclamation was sincere. She'd been trying to get me to say who I had a crush on for weeks, but I wouldn't tell her. James, of course, with his champion's smile and confident stride— the most popular boy in school, and black, which meant I was doubly cursed to remain unnoticed. He'd never leave the top social echelon of the middle school's students to date a geeky white girl, no matter how elegant a way I found to tell him, so it was best to keep my crush to myself.

"No. He's my *brother*." They stopped laughing, took a few steps away from me, their eyebrows arched, their hands half over their mouths—they did this in perfect unison, as if they had practiced it.

"Really?" Keisha said.

"Really." But they didn't believe me yet. Micah has his father's face, with the Mexican hair and eyes from our mother's side of the family—dark brown, almost black. I look just like my father, through and through. No

Latina beauty for me—blue gray eyes and pale skin. There is nothing in either of our faces that might hint we're from the same genetic pool. Finally, I was charged to prove myself by going to talk to him. Their logic: no one except family would be brave enough to talk to the strange, wild boy beneath the pine. I walked across the field at a steady pace while Keisha and the boys followed, though at a distance. When everyone was close enough to hear me, I spoke to him, perhaps more loudly than I needed to.

"Hey, Micah."

"Hey, Danielle," he said, mimicking my tone and head gesture—one of his favorite games. He didn't stop walking. I stood there for a moment, watching him walk briskly in a long figure eight, wondering what I would say to prove he was my brother. How strange to make theater of relation.

"Did Mom tell you what she was making for dinner tonight?"

"Um, no. What is she making?"

"I don't know. I was asking you."

"Oh, yeah. I don't know. I hope it's spaghetti," he said in my general direction, though not directly at my face.

"Yeah, me too." I looked over his shoulder to the amazed threesome behind, making the same shocked gestures and faces as before. My stomach sank. How strange to *have to* make a theater of relation. They should have already known he was my brother.

Ever since, Keisha liked to give me updates on Micah's progress in their biology class. I never asked her to. I knew she did this mostly out of fascination for his disorder, and partly out of affection for me. It was her way of apologizing for having laughed at him before she knew he was my brother. She would give me a list of behaviors and want me to explain them in clinical terms. I'd never read anything on autism. Like everyone else, all of my official learning about autism came from the movie *Rain Man*, which didn't explain much about Micah.

Keisha hadn't shown up in my life until that year, seventh grade English class with Ms. Hanson. We were on the "Advanced Track" for English and writing while other students in the school were placed elsewhere in the intellectual hierarchy: "On Track," "Remedial," and "Special Ed." My brother is two years older than me, but was only a year ahead of me in school and in the Special Ed class. He met with his homeroom teacher for the first half of each day, and was "integrated" into regular classrooms in subjects he could manage. This was supposed to give him experience in normative social interactions—as if middle school students anywhere were normal.

In elementary school, he'd had a small group of friends from his Special Ed class that sat together at lunch and went to each other's birthday parties. They were occasionally teased by the other kids for their strange outbursts or looming stares, but mostly they were left alone and sometimes treated kindly. But in middle school everyone was at the mercy of the masses and the masses were decidedly unmerciful: anything not status quo was responded to with humiliation or violence.

"Micah's your brother, right?"

"You already know the answer to that."

"Did you hear what happened in class today?"

"No."

"He started *freaking out*. Those mean white boys kept poking at him and calling him names and all of a sudden he started throwing things and screaming . . . everyone had to get under the desks. It was like Desert Storm up in there. He started throwing rocks, books, a microscope—no one could get him to stop."

By *mean white boys*, she meant the Sidmore boys, who'd taken to chasing him home from school, barking at him, and throwing rocks at his head. They were squinty-eyed blondes who said *fuckin'* before every noun and came to school with dirty clothes and sometimes bruised cheeks.

"Mr. Raul started yelling at him—"

"Jesus, that's the exact wrong thing to do."

"Yeah, what are you supposed to do when he gets like that?"

"I don't know. But not that."

"You don't know?"

"*I don't know*. He's got his own brain. I don't know what he's thinking all the time."

"I know what he was thinking," she said. "*I'm not gonna take it anymore.*"

"Who knows what he's thinking. Who knows how much he remembers from anything—how much he understands?"

✳

My father left the house in the middle of December my junior year of high school, and didn't come back. Everyone fell into a deep silence. Temperance was strange to all of us. It filled the spaces of the house like stars: distant, bright. Micah began to see a counselor—a specialist in high-functioning autism. I didn't pay much attention—turning inward, reading and writing in my room, concerned with the small dramas of my adolescent life.

My mother told me one afternoon that Micah told his counselor that he knew something was wrong with him—"Something is wrong with my brain," he said, tapping his temple, "and I want my brain to be better." He worked with this counselor trying to forge new neuro-pathways that would help him connect. Micah began keeping a diary of progress and a list of social goals:

> Say hello to people.
>
> Ask how they are feeling.
>
> Give someone a compliment.
>
> Wait patiently in line.
>
> When you are feeling frustrated or angry, go for a walk.
>
> Do not scream at people, hit them, or throw things at them no matter how angry you are.
>
> Do not follow Latrisse if she doesn't want you to.

Micah had a crush on a girl from his high school whom he followed around, wide eyed, everywhere she went. She was taller than him, African

American, and had more than twice his body mass. He couldn't stop telling her how beautiful she was. *Will you be my girlfriend? Will you be my girlfriend? I love you.*

But he was a joke to her. She laughed and kept laughing, until one day she asked if he had any money. He explained he received seventy-five dollars from his father for Christmas and had kept it in his bank account. She told him if he gave her the money, she would be his girlfriend. He gave her the money.

From then on, she spat at him whenever he went near her. She gathered groups of friends to jeer at him, throw dirt clods at his head. This didn't dissuade him because she had clearly stated before the exchange that she would be his girlfriend if he gave her the money, and he believed her.

My brother's love affair finally ended one afternoon when he tried to touch her shoulder to stop her from turning away and she punched him in the face, called him *retard*, and walked away laughing. He understood violence—the way it maintains the boundaries between people. He realized, if only tangentially, that he wasn't real to her. He was a boy in a movie, a story of someone else's life, a fragmented object, a spectacle.

Common symptoms of autism: impairments in verbal and nonverbal communication present from early childhood. The inability to lie (and worse, not even thinking to lie (and even worse, believing what people say (and the worst, not judging anyone for lying or telling the truth) as lies only cause confusion) because life is confusing enough). Immediacy. That is, acute awareness of sensory input. Being always in the moment. Abnormalities of social interaction: severely stunted ability to control or manipulate social interaction (lack of skill in emotional manipulation). Not mindful of the distinctions between race, class, gender, body mass, age, disability (that is, not knowing to behave differently toward people because of these distinctions). A lack of regard for social expectations. Idiosyncratic displays of confusion toward neurotypical cognitions (confusing reactions to emotional displays, dishonesty, or violence). Having too much passion for things or people: a restricted repertoire of interests. A memory full of sharp detail (directions, colors, dates, names). Repetitive acts. Repetition.

❋

Flinch away. Look in the other direction. I give you permission. Turn your head from the scene. You don't know how he'll react if he finds you watching. It's scary, sure. Of course it is. Push him to the margins of the page, as I have. Don't you feel better now? There he is on the periphery, walking in the field, beneath the pine tree. Or he is not there. He is somewhere else—farther from the line of sight. It's easy to forget him, because who knows how much he remembers—understands. He flinches away. You flinch away. It's easy to miss each other. You feel better now—don't you? It's almost as if he doesn't exist. This is easier for you. And when I say you, I mean me. Because I'm a coward. Cowardice is. Cowardice is an opening. Cowardice is an adjustable opening in one's psyche that limits. (The amount of light that can enter.)

❋

One morning, in the kitchen, Micah didn't flinch when I walked into the room. He didn't sulk, or stamp his feet, or send me sharp eyes. Instead, he stared at me, anxious. I knew this meant he wanted to speak, but I ignored him, pretended to be absorbed in pouring my cereal, milk, lifting each spoonful to my mouth, stirring my tea, smoothing my hair—anything other than give him attention. The winter light outside swirled on the glossy linoleum, and somewhere in his head he was trying to speak to me, but I didn't care. I said goodbye as I left the kitchen and he remained silent at by back.

The next morning we went through the same actions. I walked into the room and he looked straight at me, his eyes huge, direct, full of speech, but he was silent. I ignored him *who knows what he's thinking?* and attended to the same cereal ritual. All through my meal I could feel him looking at me. After I took my last bite I looked at him, and he immediately looked at his bowl of soggy cereal.

"Okay, fine. What. What is it. Just tell me. But say it quick."

"Um, Danielle."

"*Yes?*"

"Did you know that I love you?"

I stared at him. He stared back.

"I guess I figured . . . but you never said so."

"Oh. Yeah. I said it now, though."

"Yeah. Thanks."

"Because my counselor told me to write a list. See?" He pulled a badly crumpled piece of yellowed paper out of his pocket that had a short list in black ink. I was too far away to read it.

"What's it a list of?"

"People I love. See, you're here," he points to a scribble on the page, "because you're my sister and you're nice to me when Dad is mean. Remember?"

"Remember what?"

"When Dad was mean and you came to see me." I couldn't speak—light like a lump in the throat. He went on, "Oh, it's okay. It's okay if you can't remember. I remember. Yeah. It's okay if you can't remember. I was in my room, you know, on the floor. And you were there. At the door. Inside the light."

Mercy

It was a kind of mercy playing that old upright—scratched mahogany, little coffee-cup halos burned into the surface, tarnished strings pulled wrong. It was a gift from an uncle who couldn't take it with him when he moved to California: *Maybe the girls will take lessons*, but the lessons cost and we never had enough.

Each night, my mother's hands worried over dinner, slicing garlic, onion, tomato, her own fingers, and apologized to no one—to herself. I played from a worn music book, wanted to make her happy, but the songs always sounded sad, warped out of tune. So I thought of bright things as I played: sunflowers, the orange groves she wandered as a girl in California, her father's Spanish accent—his smoky laugh. My hands grew stronger and stronger, though my mother never smiled. *So beautiful!* She'd call from the kitchen—praise for anything I could barely manage: scales, or simple songs—a hymn called "Mercy."

William knew the words and sang it to me as we stood in the soaked soccer field at school, his dark hand closed over mine—the song I learned for him though he would never hear me play. When the other boys chased me, I'd show them Mercy—a game played face to face, palm to palm, fingers interlocked. The aim is to twist each other's fingers—push back on the wrists and twist until one can't stand the pain and begs, "Mercy." Whoever begs mercy first, loses. Whoever grants the mercy, wins. My father taught me. I always beat the boys at school but never won against my father.

William never wanted to play Mercy. He said we were friends and sometimes he'd bring me flowers he'd picked from yards and sidewalks: pansies, dandelions, morning glory, all wilted by the time he delivered them into my hands, without ceremony—"Here." We pretended not to know what it meant. We pretended not to know a lot of things—our stories exchanged without comment.

His father had left a few years back. I thought him lucky not to have a father, except this made his mother sad, awake at night, crying and touching William's tired eyes, the quick slope of his jaw, his soft chin, the paler creases in his dark palms—looking for signs of his father's return from *God knows where* with *some white bitch he barely knew*. My mother also cried a lot, alone in the blue light that shone through our curtains, waiting for my father to come home, talking whiskey, leaving a few bruises on her wrists, smashing a piece of furniture—proof of his arrival, his sense of mercy: he would never hit her beautiful face. Sometimes William and I were too tired to talk on our breaks and just slumped together against the concrete wall, eyes closed.

The only time I saw his apartment was on his birthday. His mother was surprised to find me, pale and skinny on her doorstep, and closed the door without saying why. I heard yelling, and finally William opened the door, let me in. His mother handed me a cupcake, told me to "keep quiet." I was the only guest. We ate our sweets against the gray wall outside his bedroom. Later, we sat on the parking lot curb, taking turns listening to the Walkman I'd given him (silver wrapping paper, silver bow) until my mother arrived in our metallic blue Chevy. I stood to say goodbye, but William was already walking away.

We didn't talk for a long while after that—drifted like loosed balloons over the school grounds until one day he found me near the cyclone fence at the edge of the soccer field where I wandered alone during lunch breaks. He wanted to play Mercy. It was early spring, still cold—our breaths a whiteness rising between us. I agreed and we walked through the muddy field to the far right corner, almost to the street, next to a telephone pole. It was as far as we could go without trouble.

We faced each other and interlocked our fingers. At the count of three, we forced each other's wrists back. He winced at first—his fingers thin and flexible—but he made his face cold as he bent my fingers deeper so that I had to bend back. Our hands strained, shook—he stared up over my head as if something hovered there. Heat gathered in my tendons. I bent his fingers harder. His arms began to tremble and his eyes welled up. I knew he didn't have the leverage to push any further without hurting himself, but he showed no sign of saying "mercy." I realized I could snap off his fingers and he wouldn't say it.

I said, "Mercy," and our hands sprung apart—floated back to our sides. He turned his back to me and shook out his fingers.

"You won," I said, but he didn't respond. "Good job," I tried again, but he flinched away—showed me only a backward glance, the hard silhouette of his face. I placed my hand on his back, between his thin shoulders, and as if pushed forward by my great, brute strength, he bolted away from me—soared a straight line over the soaked field, the wet asphalt, into a door that slammed shut behind him. I leaned forward a little, into the space he left. A beaten, gold Buick drove past slowly. The telephone wires hummed.

I go from Santa Fe to New York and New York to Santa Fe longing for wherever I'm not. Exiting the train at the Broadway stop, glancing at the still-standing buildings, I think of the way the Sangre de Cristos burn red in winter light. The first time I meet Jon, I walk away shaking (large, dark eyes). The pigeons take flight. Through the back lot, the broken glass glows. I take a class called World Religions. I can't sleep next to him, so I lean from his window, watching the sun rise on the blue and white mosque. The beggar on the corner has no arms and no legs. When we want another round, we say, *Make mommy pretty*. A famous beauty inquires about Warhol's *Electric Chair*. I dream of another life in which I am not a receptionist. Sparks rise from our limbs as we watch the skyline collapse, hold each other up like soft dolls on our vigil home. I stare a long time at the Rauschenberg collage hanging near my desk in my line of sight. We lift ice cubes from the tequila (Corazón) to our mouths, or drop them on the roof and call it hail. After, I trace the tattooed blue flames on his forearms. Instead of asking, I plant zinnias, sunflowers, love-in-a-mist. For the first time I see real Picassos, van Goghs, and I can see the brushstrokes—*I can see the brushstrokes!* But the famous beauty wonders what the electric chair means, why it's repeated four times on the faded red panel. Celine and I rename the men we are dating: *The Projectionist, The Irishman, The King of New Jersey*. I sweep my leg over the saddle of his bike and grip my arms around his waist. The shop is empty and the sky uncharacteristically gray; each time I look at the clock, only three minutes have passed. At the end of her street we can see across the channel—lower Manhattan smoking and an empty space. Through the turnstiles, I walk into an angry crowd, everyone speaking a different language and no one speaking English. I take a class called The Art of Listening. Each morning, I sweep neat piles of seeds from the terra cotta patio—throw them away. I hold him tighter than I need to, smelling his soap, sweat, the musk of his leather jacket. Jon says he still loves me, but he's leaving for San Francisco. The question of the painting pins her like a spotlight. Professor Diablo invites me to his house, pouring more tequila in my endless glass. Snow on sunflowers. Dirty water sliding down the tiled station walls. Outside, boughs reach for my open window, their veins hot. Each time I look up from my desk, I think about the black and beige shapes of that Rauschenberg—they way they almost mean. He tells me I look like the Modigliani nude he posted over his hard bed the autumn he starved in Manhattan. He works with the crew down at Ground Zero, says, "I've seen too many people die today. I need you to hold me." Los Alamos on fire. Manhattan falling down. Each night I lie awake, watching the bright green seeds of the Chinese elm outside our bedroom window fall like confetti. I take a class called Natural Disasters. Angel-bug and I drive around listening to disco in his aqua-colored car. Celine says, "Oh, we don't wait in lines," as she glides past the bouncer and through the dented metal door. I decide not to speak so as to seem mysterious. I like this vacillation between everything and nothing—the thick black smudge at the center of the painting might hide a form beneath it and I like to imagine what that is. Rain pools red at the corners, candles at the corners, the buildings peeling with the faces of lost people. I'm crying so hard I don't even know I've stepped out into traffic. The lights look small from the roof where we are slow with liquor and lean against the dark, heated slant. Professor Diablo leaves roses on my doorstep, messages crackling with flamenco music. Alone in the shop, propping myself up on an elbow, waiting for a customer to walk through the door so I'll have someone to talk to. I sleep in Erin and Emilee's computer room, grateful for the warm blue lights, the soft electric hum. Marq smokes artfully near the piñon as snow falls on his wool jacket, his wavy red hair. I take a class called *Paradise Lost*. Three mornings in a row, I wake up thinking, *If you stay here, you'll be dead in five years*. The Arabic-speaking family that owns the corner store is dragged out by police in the afternoon light. Professor Diablo shows up on my doorstep to say I should let him fuck me tonight. The sun goes down with a fight of gold, deep purple, a splash of red at the edges of hills. Lindsay is heartbroken and I don't know what to do but feed her soup and bring her blankets. I stay in the job until the end of winter, leave just after the first good thaw. Celine tells me she's fallen in love, and I know she means it when she says his real name. "I'm happy for you" (a shorn field in my voice). On the train home I realize I'm no longer in love with Jon, and although he left years ago, the absence of love surprises me. Beneath the strong black strokes on Rauschenberg's canvas, I always see a human form falling and falling. In the end, she decides not to buy the *Electric Chair*, turns, instead, to a canvas of flowers. Spring arrives in secret, and I leave for another city. The channel water glints like something sharp. I like better to imagine that it hides nothing.

Soliloquies with Strangers

Rain-slagged and weary in the back booth, I lean against the red faux leather and stare through vodka tonic to you: the queen on stage. *Lightfast* is the word for color that never fades, and I've forgotten the antonym. You shift from stiletto to stiletto, the contrapposto of your form an obvious ploy. You love the spotlight, purse your lips to it, open your wide mouth to a long, operatic soprano. The not-so-delicate fan your hand makes when you open it, palm facing the audience, strums the stiff ends of your wig. Fingernails: Chanel's Summer Fire.

Please, girl. It's February, and I'm in the dark again. Neither of us is fooling anyone. Just a few hours ago, my lover confessed, while we were still lying in my bed, that he's been with another woman the whole time I've known him. You and I, Shequida, we're just dirty secrets. So much unmarked money moved around. We're opposites of lightfast, *fugitive* in a world of color. I'm fading hourly since I punched him in the chest, dragged him naked down the stairs, said "Fuck you," and "Don't ever come back." But, Sheq, it didn't make me feel better. And I'm so sick of it, I just want to lie down in this booth and die, or else walk up to that sad, low stage and shove my fist in your mouth, tear off your glitter lashes, kick you in the balls.

The thing about being a woman, honey, is that we're all taught to hate each other—to mimic our mothers' humiliation—direct our rage toward ourselves. Take you and me, Sheq. We aren't even acquainted, but I know I could provoke you into violence just by saying something ugly. That's how potent the rage is, just under the skin. And then, after the janitor is sweeping up our hair, and the waiters are done staring and counting out their cash, you and I might sit there in the dark on the edge of the stage, holding hands, and I'd ask the color of your polish. Tell you I think it's pretty. I'd touch your shoulder softly, look into your eyes. Apologize the way a man does as he's leaving.

I know you've been bored, pretending to stare out the front toward some future customer, but the windows have fogged from the cold/heat/cold/heat and now you can't see the street. Besides, it's late. Everyone who will come here tonight has already arrived. I've thrown the soaked, faux fur coat I found in my closet when I moved into my Queens apartment onto the bar stool next to me to make some sort of large motion, so that the guy in the tux might notice me and say something. When I order my drink from you, you look at me like you know what I'm up to. He doesn't glance down from the football game on the screen looming above my head. You probably think I'm pathetic.

I think I'm pathetic, but I don't care just yet. You've twisted that frayed rag into and out of that pint glass too many times to count, and when I ask him who's playing, you smile to yourself. Most of your customers are in the back room for Celine's Red Party, all wearing red beneath the red light. Celine is now very drunk, birthday drunk, and has locked herself in a corner for some time with a boy she knows only by his face but not his name. She is part Filipina with a heart-shaped face, a smoky laugh, and a preference for sturdy blond men. I've known her six years. We like to laugh together. This boy with her in the corner is neither sturdy nor blond, but he's young and lithe with a sly, pretty face and has adored her for an achingly long time. She knows this and lets him. Like me, she lives to be adored.

He clearly does not adore me yet. His reply to my question ("So, who's playing?") is "You know anything about football?"

"No," I tell him, "but I promise charming naïveté in place of hard knowledge." You're listening—pretending not to listen—but think this is funny enough to smile. He merely smirks. You lean over the counter with my vodka tonic and I hand you my card. I think for a minute if I wasn't already half in love with this dark-eyed stranger, I'd find you appealing: pomaded hair, immediate blue eyes, forearms sleeved in koi fish tattoos.

"My team: Nebraska," he says, "and they're losing so I'm in a bad mood."

"And why is Nebraska your team?" I sip demurely from my tiny black straw, give him my best feigned interest. He's Asian, and because I imagine Nebraska a long, grassy state of German descendents, I'm surprised to hear it's the home of his team, but I don't say this. I'm afraid the sleet I walked through to get here has ruined my hair and smudged the mascara I so carefully applied before I left. Earlier in the evening, I'd wandered lost, walking in circles through the East Village for an hour—finally found the address, fumbled through the door, and walked the length of the bar to the back room, where a red glow indicated I'd come to the right place. When I walked into the room (everyone lit red and screaming drunk) he was standing there calm at the center of it, smoking, a black tux, bow tie untied like a promise.

"It's where I grew up," he says, making brief eye contact. "I know it's a bit bourgeois to like the game, but you have to understand there's nothing to do in Nebraska—just have sex and play football."

"So, you played football?"

"No," he smiles wide at his own joke and looks at my face, really for the first time, "So, where did you grow up?"

"Portland, Oregon."

"You're liberal, then."

"Radical liberal West-Coast feminist."

"I've always thought feminists are hot," he says. I laugh a bit too loudly, shocked at his bravado. He takes another drag of his cigarette and asks me another question, but you don't hear it because the ruddy-faced man at the end of the bar has raised his hand to get your attention and you're walking toward him, out of our scene, out of what (is not yet obvious) will be a wild, unencumbered mistake.

✳

I call you stranger because you want me to call you stranger. The way you stand there across the street and let the traffic between us blur my view of you, and don't raise your hand or eyes when I wave hello because you like to think yourself exotic. You want to prove it—make me feel uncertain that it's you to whom I'm waving. You like to think that I could mistake your face for any Asian face on the street, because it makes me whiter and makes you more ashamed to be with me, and the shame draws us closer—invisible rope between us.

The first time you touched me was a game and perhaps you didn't mean to mean it. But you and I are both good at games and when you drew the card I said meant you had to kiss me, now, while everyone was in the other room, you lifted me by my hips onto the white countertop beneath the pallid light in your best friend's kitchen and bit into my neck. We were both startled by the sound I made and you looked at me and I at you. Your friends walked in, carrying over some laughter from the other room, but you and I were still not breathing and when they saw us they went silent—apologized softly and fluttered out like clumsy moths.

Remember on the ride to your apartment in Long Island City, the winter sun exhausted, glinting from odd angles off the chrome bars of the train into our eyes so that we could barely see each other, and you asked me if I found you exotic? We'd been dating two months, and at first I was hurt that you might think so little of me—my feelings for you reduced to fetish. And then I realized that you must be asking because you thought *me* exotic, a fetish. It seemed to fit the games, the way I always felt (even when we were alone—especially when we were alone) we were acting out a scene in your life. Now I like to think that at moment, at that very moment, I began to exoticize you, out of spite.

You sit in the desk next to mine with your wide, watchful blue eyes waiting for me to make a mistake. You're three years older than I am and because you're an only child and lived in a sorority house in college, you feel this entitles you to give me older-sister advice when we eat lunch in. When I speak of you to Celine I use your first and last name, though we know no one else with your first name. This is to imply and that you and I are not intimates.

Our boss is a small, fair man with a mercurial disposition who likes to yell at me in the late afternoons. He especially likes the word *idiot* and leans on it when I've failed to perform any menial tasks. Thus far, I'm a terrible receptionist and you're a little sad that you convinced him to hire me and I'm sorry for that. You're good at your job and your skin is angelic. I could probably be better if I tried, but the windows open my view to other Manhattan buildings where everything is reflected and my daydreams have daily expanded to grossly unrealistic ends. Mostly, we sit side by side in silence and there's much about me you don't know. For example, since ending my tenuous romantic relationship, this job has become completely unbearable. When I enter the office each day I'm struck with nausea and blurring that dissipates immediately at quitting time. I've recognized for some time that my symptoms are merely psychosomatic, not asbestos hidden in the ceiling as I had originally surmised.

Today is the day before Valentine's Day, and I've been squinting at my computer screen and eating antacids while you repeatedly call your soon-to-be-gynecologist fiancé about the jewelry box he has not yet bought you. All morning, I've received messages from a Mister E. Hart who refuses to reveal his real name. I pretend to not know it's the man I recently threw out of my apartment. He writes, *I'm undone with the thought of you. Undone and left with nothing, your scent still in my bed*, and in my response message, I guess the names of two imaginary men he might be to insinuate I have other lovers. I laugh out loud as I write it.

"What's so funny?" you ask, pressing the phone down firmly in its cradle.

"Nothing," I say. You turn to your filing.

I wake up on the floor, shaking in the silence without you, my admirer responds.

Before it came to this, I remember laughing everywhere. What he said, I can't remember, just bright laughter like boughs of fruit. Laughing so hard I often fell to the floor, to the pavement, to the exposed roots of the trees in Central Park, into the piles of old furniture lining the streets before trash day. We'd greet each other with laughter, and walk through my doorway laughing, and laugh into the dark corner of my room where we'd transform into shifting silence (a liturgy of breathing).

The silence is breaking me. I sit quietly, hoping you'll call. But nothing.

"I find your letters tiresome," I type. "What is the point of revealing your feelings without revealing who you are?" As I write, I recall the sharp light from his high bedroom windows, and us on his bed beneath them— how, lying down, I could see only the glint of tall buildings. It's not unlike the view from my desk. One evening after the light had gone out and we were too weary to touch each other anymore, he began telling me about his childhood in Nebraska. His voice filled with hills and sky and a terrifying emptiness. Long snow drifts crept into a description of his town. Corn fields grew in the place of neighbors. He was adopted by an Irish American family from Nebraska. Despite his family's prominent position, he remained an Asian stranger in the small town where he grew up. Because he felt he should, he began dating the only African American girl at his school. His white friends asked how he could kiss her, how he could stand to touch her disgusting hair, and he worried what they must have thought of his hair.

Somewhere in this vast emotional wasteland we refer to as America is someone who will be thinking of you tomorrow.

"But the truth is, I wasn't attracted to her," he admitted.

"Then why date her—a kind of protest?"

"Maybe, but it didn't work out. I wasn't attracted, and then I was ashamed that I wasn't attracted."

"But you shouldn't have expected yourself to love the only other minority in town for that reason alone, just as you shouldn't have expected yourself to love someone from the white majority for that reason alone. Attraction isn't about politics."

"Of course it is." He looked up at the window ledge. I pressed my cheek to his neck.

"Yes, okay. They're not unrelated. I'm just saying," I tapped my fingers at the center of his chest, "there's no reason to feel ashamed."

I stood there in the cold waiting for you to gaze out your open panes. You could have me at your knees. But there was a reason for him to feel ashamed, and he felt it for me, too. I'd tell you more about it if telling you wasn't wildly inappropriate.

"Have you done the weekly grocery order yet?" you ask, leaning over my desk a little. I've been so absorbed in memory, I'm surprised to see your face. Before I can answer, you begin to lecture me, "What's wrong with you today? You keep zoning out."

I almost think you can read my screen and I feel my face turning hot. There's a tightly wound ball of rubber bands on your desk, though I feel it in my throat, my chest. I apologize to you and mean it. I want to say it over and over. I want to throw my arms around your soft neck and cry into your crisp, cream-colored blouse. I want you to you brush my cheek with the back of your hand and shush me, or for you to pull two martini glasses from your desk, fill them with burning pink, and sip slowly while I tell you everything. I want you to keep me from jumping out of the window out of sheer frustration. I'm on the cusp of doing something reckless and I want you step in without hesitation and give softly admonishing advice. *Soon the day will pass, and this torture will come to an end,* my screen tells me before I click the letter closed. I want to tell you, truly: you would have made a wonderful sister. But the phone begins to ring. I answer it.

I see your face, glassy in the window (behind it, traffic, the perpendicular of the business district, and an opaque sky bland as a beige wall), and I know you are me, but I don't recognize you. I can't recognize my face in my face—it seems an echo arriving back to me from across a wide canyon. You're sitting beside him on a dark, wooden stool in the front window of the café. You're talking about Vietnam: the way the jungle itself seemed crouched around Ho Chi Minh City, ready to, at any moment, take the city back. You've been there and he hasn't; you're trying, as always, to impress him, but as always, it isn't working. He's interrupted your American-centric observations to say he plans to go there someday to find his biological mother. On his birth certificate, the space for "biological father" is left blank. Blank usually means scandal or soldier.

It occurs to you for the first time that it might pain him to listen to you talk about the country he's spent so much time thinking about, but has never visited. It also occurs to you that he's tall for a Vietnamese man—that his face doesn't hold the classic Vietnamese features (no wide-set eyes, no round cheeks; his face is oval with a sharp chin, his eyes direct and close set)—and that since his father is unknown, it's possible that he is not all Asian. You note this because it seems his favorite topic as of late: that he is Asian. As if he were informing you of something you hadn't noticed.

Every time you are in a crowd—on the way to dinner, or jostled in a street fair—and another pedestrian bumps into him and doesn't apologize, he says, "See, I'm invisible. I'm of the invisible race." He likes to point out the Asian stereotypes in movies and books: honorable shopkeeper/family man lacking in masculine attributes, otherwise kung fu master driven by rigid ideology, but always sexless, unappealing to white women. This bothers him to an extent you find suspicious. It's as if he's pointing out your freakish attraction to him, or his freakish attraction for you.

"I'm so attracted to you, I find it disturbing," he said to you last night, then bit so deeply into your shoulder you could feel the violet-black bruise forming before he unclenched his teeth from your flesh. You like the sharp ache, then release—the way it makes you float a little over your body. You like the way it makes you feel not like you. You often think that if you were not already lying down, you might faint into a fine gray mist, into gloaming, into something observable but not quite tangible. And of course, then, you bite him back.

There's a kind of intimacy in ruin, you think as you look from your face to his face in the café window. You're thinking of your parents—your mother up late fretting at the blue curtains, waiting for your father to come home, and when he does, screaming for hours, and in the morning, flowers, silence, some piece of furniture missing, little splinters or shards of glass leftover, a bruised wrist, their eyes red from crying. Years after they'd split, when you were home from college and staying at your father's house, he told you about his first affair. He thought himself brave to return to your mother after. He thought himself brave to return to her every time.

A silence has bloomed between you now. The corners of his mouth are downturned over the cold scene outside. An Asian woman in a gray trench coat shivers at the corner. It has begun to rain and her head is unprotected. He wraps his arms around his chest, leans forward a little.

"I won't be able to see you this weekend," he tells you, "I'll be in Minneapolis, visiting my brother." Like the rest of the family he was adopted into, his brother is of good midwestern Irish stock and they are close friends. He goes up to visit him every few weeks and you find this closeness charming. They drink a lot when they're together, and you know if you call he won't answer. He promises to introduce you to his brother when he's in New York City next. You believe what he says because you want to.

Yes, I am crying on the train, and no you don't have to ask what's wrong. I'm crying for reasons other than why I am crying right now—it's a story that started a long time ago: possibly at birth. Keep staring straight past me into the shifting, subversive blackness of the subway tunnels—palpable winter humidity almost cocooning us—this is the kind thing to do. Besides, soon this downtown 6 will deliver me to the glittering world above, where the night will obscure my red eyes and the tears will shine like decoration beneath the streetlights. You think I'm romanticizing my pain, and you're right. Let me cry anyway. Let me feel how completely alone I am—more so when you pretend not to see me.

You have the weighted exhaustion of the subway lights on your face, your thick form squeezed precariously into your navy blue, polyester skirt-suit, and your curly hair frizzes out from your plastic barrette. As far as I can tell, you haven't been crying tonight but your eyes look it. You hate your job. The last man to say you were beautiful was your husband and where is he now? You have children—probably teenagers—and a mother who is sick and has opinions on everything and whom you wish would just be quiet for once and let you crawl into her arms as you used to do when you had nightmares as a child and be rocked there until you fall into a deep, deep sleep.

I'm not pretending my problems are greater than yours. I'm young, sometimes beautiful, and I'm on my way downtown to a show. Celine is working at Fez tonight so can get me in and drinks for free and she is always funny and dear. You would like Celine. Everyone likes her. She says this particular drag queen is a classically trained soprano, and is fabulous, and I must, *must*, come hear her. I will drink until cross-eyed in my own red booth and let my mind become a stained glass window through which her voice will shimmer.

"Yes, I'll come," I told Celine over the phone, sitting on my floor in front of my window where two stories below and ten minutes before, I had watched him pick up the last of the clothes I'd thrown all over the street (a shoe from beneath a car, his button-down in the bare trees like a spontaneous, overgrown flower) and the pair of old women across the street, pointing and laughing at the naked man on my stoop dressing slowly, refusing to look up at my window.

They were laughing because it was obvious what had happened. You would have laughed. I might have laughed, too, if it hadn't been me in the window, or me in the bed when he told me, while we were still naked, that he'd never marry a white woman, *ever*.

"Your family is white," I replied.

"What does that matter?"

"And I'm only half white."

"You *look* white."

"I wasn't making any plans to marry you, but just to clarify, you mean to say I'm just a fling between the last Asian girl you dated and the next?" My voice rising.

He responded by looking away at the water stain in the corner of my bedroom ceiling.

"The last girl you dated was Asian, right," I continue, "so why didn't you marry her? She was perfect according to your only apparent requirement. What broke you up—did you find out she had a German great-grandfather?"

He kept his eyes on the stain. It occurred to me suddenly that he'd never told me how he and his last girlfriend had broken up—only that she'd moved away. My heart pounded.

"Where did she move to?"

"Who?"

"Your last girlfriend." He still couldn't look at me. I grabbed his beautiful face in my hands and forced him to.

"Minneapolis," he said finally.

Yes, of course, you might think. The story seemed to be leading there. Clearly, that would be his response. And then the screaming fight, punching his chest, so enraged I pinch his earlobe like a bad child and march him and his clothes down the stairs to the street where I throw him and them out into the cold and slam the door behind me.

This is my stop. You see how trite the story is—how ridiculous I am to keep crying. I know it. You know it. *But why did you love him?* you might ask, and I'm glad that you don't because I'm already beginning to forget. Already, the love is transforming into something alien and dark. When I stand to leave, you glance up at my face with a look of deep pity, almost disgust. My display is obscene and you've suffered enough on your own. I understand why you don't want to embrace me. I don't want to embrace you, either. You look down at your worn shoes. We reflect what we both sense and don't say: we are strangers to ourselves. The door rings behind me as I step onto the tiled station floor.

I look across the street to you and my heart stammers, my eyes are whelmed, but when I blink and look again I realize you're not who I thought you were. You look like my father—brown curly hair, a little gray looped into each curl, broad face, strong nose, dark moustache above your pink upper lip. You're even wearing something he would wear on a cool Sunday after-noon—a loose, gray-blue cotton sweater, a pair of worn jeans. Your body is slimmer, less powerful, but your face and hands are deeply tanned, like his, from working long hours outside. You don't seem to notice me staring, but I suppose the slow, constant flow of taxis and cars between us—the way you disappear and reappear in my sight—is enough to distract from my fixed eyes, allow your eyes to stay focused on your confident, straight-ahead course.

I want you to look over to me, though I'd only look away in re-sponse and I don't want to look away because this act of watching is fa-miliar, almost comforting, and it's been so long since I've felt right. While I lived in your house—sorry, *his* house—I trained my eyes on his face, the menace or kindness of his gaze, like a compass I held in my mind to know which direction the day would take. He's a stranger to me now. Tell me, Dear Imposter, how love, which feels so potent and endless, changes into this sharp but distant ache—the vague shapes of a face you formerly held in your hands, the sadness of trying to remember?

I think of my mother calling, and through sobs explaining how her father had died: "His heart just stopped."

"A heart attack?" I tried, gently, to clarify.

"No. I asked the same thing, but the doctors said his heart just stopped. It just stopped."

"Can that happen?" I asked, but even as I asked, the answer was settling in the atriums of my chest. I thought of my grandfather's long, tawny limbs, the few black strands of hair that remained on his head, his sad green eyes. I felt suddenly desperate to see him again—the actual physical body of him, not a picture or voice. A few nights later, he visited me in a dream. We sat on his couch in his stucco house in East LA, the cactus plants he used to care for were gone—there was nothing on the walls. He looked cold. I placed a thick, brown blanket around his shoulders. *Gracias*, he said, then placed his great hand on my hand and said what he always said, *Daniela, be good for your mother.*

You don't care about this. I can tell by your manner—the way you amble down the street beneath the bright, dry awnings, weave around other pedestrians, certain of your movements, the strength of your form. I think of the early days of my parents' marriage, when I was very young, how he'd sometimes come home from work with a smile, flex his muscles, and yell, "Who is the strongest man in the world?" We'd squeal and run to him, hang ourselves from his arms—all four of his children hanging from his arms chanting, "You are, You are!"

The physical was important to him, which is why he was vain, and why he liked to tease my mother about her strong hips—her short, thick, Mexican thighs, her small breasts, the swell of her belly left from carrying four children to term. She was shy about her looks, made more so by his provocations, but I always thought she was lovely, wished I looked like her instead of him.

"But you *look* white," my lover liked to remind me when we were still together, his observation part of a widely accepted belief—what you see is what you get. And perhaps he's right. I always felt too much like a fraud to argue, and perhaps it was never even worth the discussion. You've already walked on, down two blocks, are hardly visible anymore from where I stand at the corner, not sure of which direction to take. You turn left, out of sight, and I'm so tired that everything begins to blur—the smudge of traffic on the road, the hazy quiver of branches, the faces of other people growing vague, forgettable, blending with other faces, with the smeared awnings and brownstones, the fragmented furniture at the curb, the slow fall of leaves from the indistinct trees, the dazed skyscrapers on the near horizon, a muddy run of mascara in the road.

This is the third night I've walked into your hardware store and asked you to help me find something. I can tell you're skeptical. You want to ask what I'm building, and to tell you the truth, I don't know. To tell you the truth, my heart is broken and now I want to build something. You *should* be skeptical. I'm a carpenter's daughter, but it's been too long since we spoke on good terms, and I can't call him for carpentry advice. I want to build a desk, maybe a picture frame for the painting I've had rolled up in my closet since I moved here. You are always just about to close when I arrive. I'm sorry for that.

I get here as soon as I can. Each night you turn paler and paler beneath your fluorescent lights and the waning winter light of New York City. Your aisles are narrow, stacked from floor to ceiling and I wander as if through a labyrinth, not understanding your order of things: washers next to hammers next to hinges next to shovels next to twine. You look nothing like him, but your accent reveals you as Vietnamese and I meditate on this as I walk numbly, looking for the handsaws.

A year ago, I was lost in the tailors' district in Ho Chi Minh City—the streets so bright with intricate fabrics that though it was all strange to me, I didn't feel afraid. Everywhere through storefronts and kiosks people were waving out cloth, smoothing cloth, billowing it down in great silk and cotton swaths, pulling it taut between themselves, lifting it from or to piles of other fabrics: blue, fuchsia, scarlet, sweet lime, mango, violet, patterned with flowers, trellises, dragons, elephants, pitchers of water—as if everyone were performing an elaborate dance to a music I could only almost hear.

I understand my impression of that day is ridiculous—that you are most likely from another city, another region of that country—that there is pain and suffering there as everywhere, but I want you to tell me something. I want you to explain how I might resolve my heart, or how to build a wooden box. Explain to me how I could be so blind, how I could let him twist me into this—for what? Yes, *for what*, exactly—and also how do I make sure the joints match up, and do you recommend glue or nails or both?

You're skeptical, and so am I. I bring my handsaw to your counter. Ring me up, and don't be afraid to admonish me for my bad romantic decisions. Tell me in another language—if you can, in the bright dialect of my memory—so that even if it's an unbearable truth, it sounds somewhat, distantly beautiful.

Still Life with Oaks

At first our eyes are drawn to oak branches moving in the wind, cresting green toward the sky and the light that is broken as it falls through them. We can see the tree from half-exposed root to pinnacle leaf. The light falls, not as arrows but as shifting net—drops, scatters, drags over the scene. Light and wind and branches. These are the only things that move. There is a hill of stiff August grass jutting out from the front porch of a small blue house (where we are playing). The hill forms a steep slant to the sidewalk—the sidewalk that stretches on and on through the city without end. The old woman next door walks out of her house and across her yard, raising her arms and calling my mother's name, "Cecilia," to ask her a question, "Cecilia?" but never asks it. Instead, she trips (*just a trip, just a trip*), tumbles down the hill, lands hard on the sidewalk, face on the sidewalk, arms splayed out on either side of her. Outside of the scene there is a walnut tree my father has not yet cut down—the only evidence of its existence here is the black and ochre smears on the cement (green fruit smashed to its hard, walnut core by listless children (angry) (latent with violence)). One of these smears rests lightly (a sleeping blackbird, a shadow) beneath her old-woman hand that I imagine might, at any moment, reach up.

The too-large red cardigan she often pushed reflexively up to her elbows is splayed open on the sidewalk as if she'd lain down to nap and the tree placed a small red blanket on her back. She's facedown on the pavement, her legs twisted unnaturally, and her white hair seems to breathe without her. Pieces of her shattered glasses scatter on the pavement (glass and light) and I think of how she might need them when she gets up, though blood has begun to pool (a small leak in a water balloon, the way the weight of itself presses the water out) near her face. We can't yet see this. The hill slants down and the tree rises up so that she lies like a nest in a valley. We are young. We think this is a game. My mother has not yet turned around to see. We hover over her like hummingbirds (attracted to red?)—slight, alighted on nothing.

I'd been his confidant and keeper for years, so when I found him in his room sitting on the floor, his knees pulled up to his chest and his face in his hands, I knew to approach him slowly. I walked in just to the center of the room so that he might look up and notice me standing there—see me in his space so that he could decide to make the first move toward connection; so that he had the power to decide; so we might retain the trust we'd so carefully built between us. He sensed me near and looked up to appraise me. He was bleary eyed and exhaustion rested over his square face in a film of sweat—the skin on his broad, tanned forehead and nose shining. The last of a rolled cigarette burned lightly in its tray on top of his wooden dresser. Another bad sign: he never smoked in the house. When he saw me standing there he didn't look surprised. Exactly the opposite. He looked expectant—burdened with the expectation of my arrival and finally sad at the fulfillment of that expectation. He looked out of the bedroom windows toward our backyard, where the garage and the neighbor's pine (too tall to fit into the window frame, jutting up past it into the uncertain sky) seemed a painted landscape.

"Good," he said softly, with an air of finality. "Good. You're here. I need to tell you something." He sniffed and wiped his nose with the back of his hands, as if to put an end to crying, but when he tried to rise up he began sobbing again and stumbled back down into the same stance: his muscular body almost fetal against the bed, his face in his hands, his hands on his knees. He had on the simple work jeans and white T-shirt he often wore on the weekends—the clothes I would always imagine him in years later and for the rest of my life. He cried harder now, I think, partly in shame for crying in front of me. I stayed still and small, my feet together and my arms next to my sides, clasping my hands in front, but not tightly, looking at the floor between us so that if he happened to look up at me in the middle of his display he wouldn't feel more shame at my having witnessed it directly—so that I could raise my eyes to meet his gaze at exactly the same moment. Several times he tried to get up in this way, and several times he didn't succeed.

I wondered how much of his distress was due to physical withdrawal (he'd gone out last night—so, cocaine and alcohol, probably both in large quantities), how much was due to true emotional distress, and how much of that distress was solvable. I knew his history by heart (nonaffectionate mother and stepfather, biological father alternately absent and abusive, family history of mental illness leading to drug abuse and suicide, aggrandized nostalgia for his high school popularity, desperate need for approval disguised by romanticized self-reliance, sexually active since age 14, addictive and violent tendencies since age 16, his forced obedience of others conflated with loyalty and love), but it was premature to judge this particular situation without at least a conversation, and that couldn't happen until he stopped crying. I wondered whether my going over to him and placing a hand on his back might have a comforting or escalating effect. Outside, the pine shivered a little, and in my peripheral view, I could sense its movement in the mirror behind me. He breathed heavily into his hands, rubbed them up over the dark brown and gray curls on his head. He looked out the window again.

That he indicated my presence was necessary to whatever narrative had led him into this state—that he "had something to tell me"—indicated that he might misunderstand a comforting gesture as affirmation of his narrative, or worse, cause further anxiety via my close physical proximity to his emotional display. It probably goes without saying that men often feel shame when crying, and this particular man, who often displayed an extra flourish of machismo—he is always the *alpha male*, he would say— found it particularly shameful to be in this utterly vulnerable state. He was a construction worker: worked hard, played hard, and his social behavior was reinforced by the equally "manly" men of his trade. Most of this identity of masculinity was anchored in his superior (yet *merciful*, he would claim) orientation above women in the social hierarchy of his world, and in dominating women—verbally, physically, sexually. He looked past me into his own face in the mirrored closet door, then rose slowly from the ground, took the few small steps past me to the mirror-closet, and slid it open. There he knelt down and rummaged through the dark mess inside and pulled out a small wooden box. He opened the box and pulled out a thick roll of what appeared to be twenty-dollar bills wrapped in a white rubber band and a piece of paper with his handwriting scrawled across. I didn't want to know what this was about anymore.

"What's wrong?" I asked, probably too late.

"Listen up. I need you to do something for me. Can you do something for me? Okay? Be a good girl and do something for me." He began to cry again, his voice breaking, but he shook his head and came out of it. "This letter has important instructions. I'm leaving it in this box in the closet. Right down here, okay?" He placed the box in the back left corner of the closet. "I'm going to leave soon, and I'm not coming back. I need you to stay calm, no matter what Mom does, okay? And I need you to find this letter and read it—it has all the instructions on what to do next: where the insurance policy is, and how much to spend on my burial. Don't show your mom the money until she starts to make funeral arrangements—otherwise, she'll spend it—okay? And don't let her buy me anything fancy, just a plain pine box. The whole point of this is to have enough to live on, so don't spend it on my death. It won't be me then: I'll just be meat. Just have them put my dead meat in a pine box . . ." At this point, he covered his face with his thick hands again and trailed off into soft, almost inaudible weeping—the long, strained notes pulled taut over the room. I shifted from foot to foot—reached out my hand and let it hover over his back, not touching.

"Where are you going?"

"I'm going to kill myself."

"Why are you going to do that?"

"Because we're broke and I can't do it. I'm working three jobs, *God damned*, and I can't do it. I was looking at everything—the finances—and I'm just worth more dead than alive. But I need to make it look like an accident: the policy doesn't cover suicide. I figure I'll walk into traffic, or . . . I don't know. I'll kill myself and it will buy some time. A few years."

"A few years?"

"A few years."

"But what happens when the years are over?"

"*I don't know,*" he said, incredulously, "I'll be dead." He knew this wasn't a good answer. He fell to the floor again, and I took a few steps back. He lay, knees to chest, with both arms stretched out so he could touch my pale, bare feet with his hands and began chanting, through labored breath, "I'm sorry I'm sorry I'm sorry," then "Please forgive me, forgive me, I can't do this anymore." This was worse than his usual Saturday morning, hungover melancholy. I tried to keep calm, but my stomach sank. In our conversations lately, he'd mentioned suicide flippantly. It had become part of his humor when talking to other adults in his circle—*worth more dead than alive* had become a kind of punch line to the end of a long day of work. As my father lay there on the floor, weeping, I imagined him and his coworkers ending a day at the job site—covered in dirt and chalking—little clouds of dust rising from their jackets where they pound each other on the back with one hand, holding their empty lunch boxes and thermoses in the other. One (perhaps a man with red hair and a big nose and handlebar moustache) might say something about a big payday, and my father might say something like, "The only big payday I'll get is the day I die."

I'm lying, of course. I didn't think of my father's friends. It is more than a little disingenuous to say I did or thought any of this consciously. I was ten years old. By now it was habit. For years he'd been vacillating between violent rage and simpering vulnerability, so I'd had years to perfect my approach. I moved by instinct—thought of nothing but what was unraveling before me. And, of course, I was terrified. I was too terrified to speak, or even cry, afraid I might do the wrong thing and speed his plans. But I remember clearly that I looked up at myself in the mirror, standing there in my bare feet—my skinny girl legs and pink shorts, my too-small T-shirt and stringy hair. I saw myself standing straight and my father on his knees with his face to the floor and thought, "I'm just a kid. I don't know how to do this."

I could hear the television from the living room, where my youngest sister, Mileah, and older brother, Micah, were on the couch, watching their Saturday afternoon programs. The quick excitement of the announcer's voice indicated some kind of advertisement. Our mother had gone to the grocery store. This morning, Jasmine, the other middle child, scavenged through the kitchen drawers, found a deck of red cards—an intricate pattern of embellishment on each back—and threw them randomly onto our coffee table, planning to sketch their shape where they fell. This was her usual weekend project. Though I couldn't hear her, I knew she was where I left her: slouched over a pad of paper with her fine lead pencils, placing quick, small strokes onto the page.

The answer occurred to me then: I could be a kid—gain his sympathy for my vulnerable position. I already looked the part, but I wasn't sure of the phrasing. I thought of what a child in a movie might say, placed my hand on his back, and said it:

"I love you, Dad. I don't want you to die. Please don't do it." It was my best shot. He began crying harder when I placed my hand on his back and my pulse trembled wildly in my throat, afraid I'd said the wrong thing. But his weeping came suddenly to a stop, and he sat up a little.

"I'm so tired," he said.

"Maybe you should go to sleep."

"Yeah, maybe I should."

I tugged on his arm a little and he wobbled into a slouching stance, threw an arm over my bony shoulder, then pressed me into his chest, hugging me so tightly I couldn't breathe. After a moment he released me and took the few short steps to the bed, letting himself land heavily on the water mattress (the resulting waves) and closed his eyes almost immediately. I pulled the red comforter from the floor and threw it over him, leaned down to kiss him on his cheek. He reached his great paw out from under the comforter and grabbed my hand.

"Don't tell your mom about this," he said.

"Okay."

"Okay." He released my wrist and let his hand go limp. I tiptoed out of the room and shut the door lightly behind me. In the living room, Mileah and Micah were on the couch, staring deep into the television. Jasmine looked up from her drawing.

"What's wrong with Dad?" she asked.

"He's tired. He's taking a nap."

"Oh."

She went back to her drawing. She'd already outlined the shape of several cards, some face up, some face down, and traced their shapes lightly with the fine lead of her pencil. Because the cards followed no particular pattern, they left empty space where the wood grain of the coffee table was exposed, and she drew this as well. She could sit there for hours, days, doing exactly this: drawing right up to the edge of the paper, creating a frame around her small chaos. Everything she created looked astonishingly real.

Summer
Pageant

We're in my backyard and Melissa insists on being The Bad Mommy, again. Her reasoning is that she's better at it than anyone else. No one argues with Melissa. She is small and pretty—brown hair, blue eyes, dimples in a heart-shaped face—but has a way of making herself bigger, of getting what she wants. She is a year older than I am, and now that I've graduated from the first-grade annex and will have a proper second-grade classroom in the main brick building of Beach Elementary, she likes to tell me what to expect, and what to do.

So Melissa gets to play The Bad Mommy and I will be The Good Best Friend because no one else wants to be. There's only one leading role left: The Baby. Everyone else will have to play The Neighbors. We choose Christina to play The Baby because she's the smallest and is best at looking scared. My little sister, Jasmine, and Christina's cousin Shari will have to be The Neighbors. They form a line down a seam in the concrete and lean out of their imaginary windows as if deeply bored. The game starts when Melissa holds up her hand out in front of her, miming a small mirror, and picks up a thin, steel-colored rock to start chopping and separating the imaginary cocaine into perfect lines.

"Did anyone bring a straw?" No one did. She pretends to roll up a dollar bill and places it to her nose—a sharp inhale. She shakes her head and grunts, wipes her nose with her fingers, then does another line like the first. Christina, The Baby, walks into the imagined living room, against the garage, just below our shredded basketball hoop.

"Mommy, what are you doing?"

"Nothing, baby, go take a nap."

"But Mommy, I'm hungry," Christina whines, "my tummy is all empty." Christina is small, even for a kindergartner, so it's especially convincing when she says this.

"Goddamnit! What did I tell you? Leave me alone!" Melissa says, rising like a tide over Christina.

"But what will I eat?"

"Eat shit!"

Christina begins her baby cry.

"Shut up or I'll give you something to cry about."

Christina cries louder, so Melissa dives over and slaps her—that is, she claps her hands near Christina's face, and Christina jerks her head in response, then places her own hand on her cheek and looks up at Melissa in mock horror. She pretends to cry softer—her green eyes magnified through her thick, pink plastic glasses; her reddish hair, as usual, a mess.

"Why did you hit me, Mommy?"

She backs herself up against our chain-link fence and looks wildly around her—begins to paw at the matted August grass that edges the concrete. We like it when Christina plays The Baby because she looks so convincingly hurt.

"Quit being such an ungrateful little *bitch*!" Melissa says this loudly, then breaks character for a moment to see if there are any adults in earshot. There aren't. She looms over Christina, raising her hand as if to strike again. Christina coils down, leaving a hand up over her face in defense. That's my cue.

"Melissa, what are you doing?!" I'm the rational, sober friend—someone like my mother. Melissa pretends to ignore me for a moment. "Don't hit your baby!" I place my hand on her shoulder now. "Have you been doing drugs?" Melissa turns her back to both Christina and I. I lean down to scoop up Christina's tiny body in a hug, and she shakes against me, whining like a hurt puppy. "You're not supposed to hit your baby! Don't you care about your baby?!"

That's when the chorus starts.

Jasmine and Shari, who are really just waiting their turns to play The Bad Mommy (everyone's favorite role), begin scolding Melissa from the windows of their pretend houses. Because they are the neighbors, they disapprove in rapid, overlapping shouts: "You shouldn't hit your babies!" "We're gonna call the cops!" "You're mean! You're gonna get in trouble!" "You're a bad mommy!"

"I can't hear you!" Melissa says loudly in our general direction.

"Melissa, look at me!" I'm trying to coax her into turning around.

"No," she says, her voice breaking.

"I'm your best friend. You can look at me," I say. At this point I let go of Christina and rise to my feet. Christina wraps herself around my right leg, cartoonishly frightened, and I try to walk over to Melissa while weighted down with Christina. Shari laughs. I look over my shoulder and give her my best glare and she goes back to being a neighbor, alternately angry and bored. Melissa has turned around now, and faces me with a scowl.

"Your eyes are all red. You are *high*," I pronounce, and The Neighbors gasp with self-righteous disdain.

"Shut up! You think you're so good? You used to do it, too!" Another gasp from the neighbors. I shake my head.

"But I stopped. Because I was so mean when I did drugs and I care about my babies." All The Neighbors nod in approval. It's time for The Bad Mommy's tantrum.

"Oh, you think you're such a good little missy. You think everything's sooooo easy. But it's not easy. *It's not easy*. It's hard. *Everything is hard all the time*." Her face is twisted into someone older and she punches the air.

"And don't ask me for anything because we don't have the money, and we'll eat when I say we eat! We'll eat then, you little bitch you stupid little bitch and *fuck you* if you can't take it. *Fuck you fuck you fuck you!*" She picks up a rock and catapults it into The Neighbors' yard, then picks up another as if she's aiming for me. I move quickly toward her, grab her shoulders and begin to shake her, my heart pounding. She tries to push me away, and I slap her. A real slap. The vague red outline of my hand flares up on her face. For a moment she's stunned. Then she looks straight at me and slaps me back—the sudden sting of the thwack, then I feel my cheek turning hot. Something in me is unloosed.

"You can't keep doing this," I say, but my voice sounds low, strange to me.

"I can do whatever I want," Melissa says.

"But you're ruining your life."

"I don't care."

"You're ruining your life."

"I said I don't care. I don't care!"

"You're ruining your life you're ruining your life you're ruining your life!" My eyes are closed now and Melissa's voice, high, shrill, finds a way over mine: "I don't care I don't care I don't care I don't care." We're screaming so loud we don't hear the back door open, or notice my mother approaching.

"Danielle! Melissa!" She shouts us out of our trance, "What's going on here?!"

All of us are shocked to see my mother standing there. We have nothing to say for ourselves.

"What are you kids doing?" she says, softer now, more concerned. Christina's eyes start to well up a little: she thinks we're in trouble. Shari walks through her invisible windows toward the gate. There's a long silence.

"Just playing," I finally tell her.

"What are you playing?"

"Just a game we made up . . . I don't know."

My mother tilts her head to the side as she assesses me and her long, dark hair hangs down past her hips. Her arms are crossed over her chest, but she looks hurt.

"It doesn't look like a very fun game to me," she says, then more carefully, "it doesn't look like a game at all."

I can't agree or disagree. We call it a game. We don't know what else to call it.

"Well . . . just . . . find another game to play. And don't hurt each other . . . or *pretend* to hurt each other." She stands there a moment to let this sink in. We nod our heads automatically. She turns away, walks slowly up the warped back-porch stairs and into the house, closing the door softly behind her. We stand silent a long while, like a cluster of small, dark marbles. Then everyone turns away.

Muse

I'm in a pleather jumpsuit, wearing four-inch spiked heels, and my short hair is down, mussed. At the edge of my view, I can see the frayed tips of my newly dyed hair swirling out—blue, purple, black—like someone else's hair. I'm sitting on a stool in a bathtub, the curtain drawn way back so that the photographer can capture me at his leisure. I have a crush on him—just a mild one, born out of loneliness and a fascination with the exotic. He's French. When he thinks he has a good shot he says *beautiful* in his French accent. His face is so unimportant, I can barely remember it from moment to moment and bright lights on scaffolding shine directly into my eyes, blur this memory. The artist—my band mate and the man who is funding this shoot—stands behind the photographer, smoking. He's so deep in shadow, he's almost a shadow himself, except for his voice.

"You look like a little pleather biscuit," he tells me, which means I look hot, edible. My heart is so broken, and the suit is so tight, I can barely breathe. "Let's turn on the shower, slick her up." The sound system in the next room blares our album on repeat, and I can hear my own voice, veiled through synth effects, singing the last lyrics of the last song: *just let it change, just let it change.* All of the mids have been engineered out of my voice so that it sounds hollow, distant, as if I were singing within a tin tunnel.

"I don't really think this is the look you're going for," the photographer says, all of his consonants soft as croissants. "You don't want to try too hard on the first album cover. It's like an introduction. You don't want to say, *Hello, we are way too cool for you.*"

I agree with the photographer. I feel more than a little ridiculous. But the artist has been one of my best friends for the past five years, and it's his money we're spending, hand over fist, in this shoot. I wonder if peeling off the pleather will take as long as it did to put on. Deep in the shadows I know the artist is wearing one of two outfits, both of which he might be seen in on any occasion, but I can't remember which he's wearing today: either paint-spilt jeans and a white T-shirt, or a black Gucci suit. Either way, his long black hair is pulled back in a ponytail, and he is looking out through his thick, goggle-like Gucci glasses.

"No way, man," the artist says, "this is hot. Everyone likes hot. Let's turn on the shower and she can throw back her arms like that scene in *Flashdance.* You know that scene, D?" The album starts over and I can hear the dance rhythm of the first song beat hard. I know if I were in the next room, it would vibrate my heart through my thin chest.

"No," I tell him.

"The one at the club?"

"I've never seen *Flashdance.*"

"How old are you?" The photographer asks. I tell him my age.

"Ah, she's a baby," he replies.

"A baby biscuit," the artist says, and they both laugh. They are both a decade older than me. From the other room, my voice sings *there's a story in every sky and every star shines alone.*

"And she is sitting right here, so you can talk to her like she's in the room," I tell them.

"Ah, my little feminist," the artist says.

"It's not feminist to want you to talk to me like I'm here—it's just good manners."

"You don't want to be objectified. I get it."

"Danielle, look at me." I lift my eyes in the direction of the photographer's voice, deep into the center of a hot white light. I hear a click and a flash emerges from it. "In art," he says, "everything is object."

When the ivory arrived, Pygmalion didn't think of it much. He hadn't sculpted anything in a while, and was sick with disdain for the models he usually used—all marred in some way. It's not that they weren't beautiful by usual standards, but that they lacked a certain purity. When he felt their bodies to measure the curves for his sculptures, he could feel other men's hands, like a palimpsest of past lovers, burning in their skin. He wanted someone completely new—someone clean. He kept the virginal bundle of ivory wrapped in its bland cloth, leaning against a corner of his studio for weeks while he stood in the opposite corner, looking out of the window over Cyprus, and beyond Cyprus, where the naked ocean rolled and rolled lewdly in its bed.

He couldn't sleep. Instead, he sat at the edge of his divan trying to envision a woman born completely grown. Not out of the filthy entry of another woman who ruined herself to beget her, but of something else. He didn't know what. Athena burst out of her father's head to be born—something like that, but less gruesome. Born, perhaps, not out of the physical brain, but out of an idea itself—a vision—like a sculpture. A light sweat arose on his forehead. His heart pounded. Suddenly, he ached to touch the ivory.

We're leaning over the console and he's pushing the switches up and down, trying to get the right equilibrium. Occasionally a box elder beetle crawls onto the surface of the board and walks lazily around the grid of knobs.

When this happens, the artist grabs a can of pressurized oxygen, and aims it at the bug, blowing it away.

"Hasta la vista," he says, laughing lightly. I laugh with him. Our friendship is new, so our conversation and gestures are tentative. When I arrived, his fiancée, M., left for a walk with their poorly behaved mutt. I apologized for interrupting her afternoon, asked her to stay for the session.

"No, that's fine. I need to go for a walk anyway," she'd said, looking not at me but at their messy kitchen counter, and slipped out of the front door with their mottled white and brown dog gnawing on his leash.

When I'd made plans to play with the artist, I'd hoped that M. and I would also be friends. But most of the time when I arrived, she'd be gone already. I hadn't seen her for months and was surprised at how much weight she had gained—her heart-shaped face was swollen, her arms thick. When we'd met, not a year ago, she was a whip of a woman. It was her twenty-third birthday and the artist had hosted a party for her in his huge warehouse studio. My boyfriend, Jon, and I had arrived late, when the party was already loud and busy. It took me a minute to adjust to the dimness of the room, and then I saw a crowd of people, all dressed much smarter than me, and the long table—about twice the length of my living room—covered with platters of food and bottles of vodka and red wine, all half-empty. The artist approached us, leading a nymph-like woman by the crook of her elbow. She smiled blithely and swooned over in her leather pants—her short, hot pink hair flipped out just so.

"You know Jon. And this is Danielle," the artist said. "Danielle, this is M." She half-lunged forward on her tiptoes and planted a sweet greeting kiss on my cheek, grabbing onto my shoulders to keep from falling over. "I've heard all about you! You're Jon's little girl!" she said, breathing vodka into my face.

"Yes?"

"Oh, I didn't mean that to be condescending," she said sincerely. "It's just that I was the little girl for so long. I'm glad to have someone else take the title. You sit near me. I won't let the other girls bully you." She leaned in conspiratorially and whispered, smiling, "They can be real bitches."

I'd already heard about the romance between the artist and the nymph from Jon. When they met, she was a teenager—a runaway from Utah—and he was twenty-two. He'd dropped out of high school to immerse himself completely in the Santa Fe art scene, but found there wasn't much work for real artists. He was half-Spanish, half-Hopi, and saw clearly the bright white lust for Native American art, so began creating and selling traditional Hopi kachina dolls to tourists. He made a good living at it for a while until, finally, a gallery agreed to show his paintings. They were huge panels of brilliant mash-ups between traditional Hopi and mainstream American figures: dolls and dollar bills, coyote tricksters and Armstrong landing on the moon, and always bright Hopi butterflies skimming through the collaged scenes. The gallery split the profits with him fifty-fifty. He sold out on opening night and bought M. a car. She dropped out of high school and helped him organize his business, working alongside him in his studio, going with him to business dinners with increasingly wealthy patrons—*clients* he called them. Years passed, and the scandal of her age slipped into so many emptied bottles of wine.

When they first came together, his friends and their girlfriends disapproved, not only because she was so much younger, but because (they patiently explained to him and then to her) she was fat. She lost weight. Then she gained it back. Then she lost weight again. Each time she carved herself back to her girlish figure, the artist would buy her another outrageous rocker wardrobe and they would go out all over town, spilling fabulous drinks on their expensive clothing. When she gained the weight back, no one would see her for months.

"Is M. okay?" I asked the artist once she was gone. He shrugged.

"Yeah, she just gets down sometimes. But she's fine."

"Is there something going on, or is she really just down?" He looked out of the window, slightly rounded to fit the curve of the adobe wall. Instead of curtains, dried rose bouquets hung down unevenly from the top window ledge—pale reminders of anniversaries and fights. Another beetle crawled across the on/off button. He still held the oxygen can in his right hand as he flicked the bug away with his left.

"Maybe both," he said, thoughtfully, "it's my fault, a little bit. Her fault, a little bit."

"What do you mean?"

"Oh, I don't know. She's been wishing lately that she'd finished high school. And I get that. But she made that decision—I didn't force her— and now she's feeling like she doesn't have a life outside of me. She wants her own career. And I get that, too. But she's gotta do something about it . . . just . . . relationships. All that shit. You know?"

"Yeah," I said, but I didn't.

He started working while the night still hung like a black tarp over the city, smoothing his hands over and over the thin columns of ivory, trying to feel the bones beneath the bone. Finally, he took a sharp palm tool and began carving toward her form in long strokes. She began to take shape in his mind: she would be small and light and round—her modest thighs barely two tusks thick, her wrists as pale and delicate as jewelry. As he worked, his eyes felt fevered, anxious to rest on her cool body. When he liberated the rough shape of her left knee from its ivory casing, he smoothed it away with the circling of his thumbs, then gently etched each fine line of her skin until the knee was a perfect fit for his tense hand. He closed his eyes and wrapped his hand around her small, faultless knee, feeling dazed—a sudden rush of heat to his groin, his head. Something in him unlocked. He undressed.

For five days and nights he worked this way—naked and wild, refusing food or drink, deepening his obsession by emptying himself of all other wants. His servants tried to enter the room, and when he wouldn't let them enter, they hovered at the threshold, their ears to the door, whispering to each other. At first, he used the carver roughly, grunting as he opened the bone, tearing away the excess material until he found the shape of her whole form. Then he used the circular strokes of his bare fingers to wear the ivory down, breathing over each part of her skin, marrying the seams of her until she was seamless. Then he used his tongue to polish her skin smooth—smoother than any blemished woman. Last, he etched her face patiently with the fine tip of a feather—her expression eternally grateful. When she was complete, he lifted her up—small and light and round— and lay her down in his bed, threw a thigh over her thighs, an arm across her arms, and fell into a deep, dreamless sleep.

※

I'd flown into Albuquerque from DCA the night before and was coming down with a bad cold, which always seemed to be the case when I came back for studio time. The artist had moved from his small first house to a larger house with an extra room where he could set up his own music studio. The new engineering console was impressively large and took up about a quarter of the room. He'd bought all new mics and filters, a new full-size piano keyboard with weighted keys, and speakers that looked as if they might, at any minute, rocket themselves into the atmosphere. I sat down, limp and fevered, on his red leather couch as he dragged recording equipment out of the small room, taped large foam pads to the walls and floor to absorb any excess sounds.

"You just sit there, Miss D, and think about what you're going to sing."

When I awoke that morning, I'd stared at myself in the mirror for a long time. My eyes were puffy and my face ashen. I opened my mouth wide and saw blisters at the back of my throat. I sipped the honey-ginger tea the artist had bought me on our ritual run to the coffee shop. While I was in town and with the artist, I never paid for anything. I kept a running receipt in my head, wondering if I'd ever be able to repay him. Last night's dinner cost him, I was sure, well over two hundred dollars. He took me to the best restaurant in town, where they didn't print prices on their menus, and ordered us a brilliant Cabernet that I was sure I'd never taste again in my life unless he paid for it.

The artist and I had shared peculiarly similar childhoods: violent, addict father, two younger sisters we felt we had to protect, and aching poverty. And we were both the *special* children, the favorites. We were supposed to save everyone. He'd been successful, but was hoping for something more stable, more definitive than the next gallery opening. He was showy with his money because he believed it attracted the wealthy patrons, but sometimes this gamble didn't work and he'd accrue debt. Feast or famine. My wealth was still as it had always been: nonexistent. Over dinner, we talked about what we would do with the money from our first album contract: we'd buy our mothers houses, pay off our sisters' bills, and go on a long European vacation. Somehow, it seemed possible, sitting in the luxe restaurant with its mannered waiters and ridiculously priced cuisine. It seemed possible that we could both rise up from our collective mire of insecurities and become what our child selves had imagined—our beautiful, future selves—that we could become different people entirely.

It was our ritual psychological makeover, and dinner was part of that ritual. Early on, M. would often accompany us, but after a particularly drunken evening in which the artist and I kept laughing louder and louder as she fell more and more silent, she stopped coming. I saw her very rarely after that. I'd worried that we'd made her jealous. The artist assured me that she was just busy and shut me down the way he always did when I tried to ask about their relationship. He never told me how their connection was deteriorating until he called me to tell me that they'd split.

"Why?" I asked, shocked.

"Because I'm in love with you," he'd told me in his joking voice.

"No, *really*, why?" There was a long pause on the other end of the line.

Finally, he said, "Eleven years. We just grew apart. There was nothing more we could do."

And I believed him, because I wanted to believe him. I looked around the room as the artist taped a foam pad to the last window, shutting us up in darkness and silence. Like a bomb shelter. Like an asylum. He took off his dark jacket and sat down next to me on the couch, a shadow in the shadows.

"Are you ready to sing for me?" Neither of us moved to flick on the lamp. For a second, I thought he would kiss me. My throat stung sharply as I swallowed down the last of my tea.

"Yes," I told him, because I wanted to believe myself.

✦

Pygmalion awoke next to his ivory virgin, and felt a flush of love for what he'd created. Immediately, he began to attend to her every imagined wish: dressing her tenderly in luxurious fabrics, brushing her unyielding hair, bringing her rich foods and gifts of bright shells and polished stones, flowers and beads, and music. He hung earrings on her ears and pearls between her pale breasts. Each night, he'd lay her down on the softest feather pillows to sleep next to him, calling her Galatea, his wife. Some nights he could hardly sleep watching the moonlight over her perfect skin, her limbs and torso latent with motion, as if, at any moment, she might breathe.

Months passed. It was the time of the festival of Aphrodite. Pygmalion was pulled out of his dreams by the sweet and musky scent of incense blown by ocean wind from the goddess's holy shrine. Because he couldn't bring his Galatea with him, he left her to nap on his bed, and walked down to the festival at the shore where young men and women were dancing in circles around the goddess's temple. The stairs to her monument were long and covered in flower petals, and as Pygmalion ascended them, he felt the graveness of his request grow heavier and heavier in his bones. When he finally reached the top, he knelt before Aphrodite's marble likeness and lit the three torches at her feet. He humbly and silently prayed to Aphrodite for a wife like his ivory virgin. Deep in her marble likeness, Aphrodite heard Pygmalion's mind, and to show her favor, breathed into the lit torches, causing the flames to explode up into a hot point and shower Pygmalion in sparks.

I hadn't slept for three nights, sinking deeper and deeper into a state of half-waking delusion. I'd been blinking at the darkness on the other side of my window for hours, waiting for my unconscious to pull me under and put me out of my misery. But just as I started to relax, sink a little, my leg would jerk—kicking me awake. Physicians refer to this as the "hypnic jerk"—normal, but unexplained. Some theorize it's the brain misinterpreting muscle relaxation for falling; you kick to catch yourself. Some think it's the brain confusing falling asleep for dying—a death twitch. *Falling. Dying. Misinterpretation.*

It was February and I was in the bell jar. What began as a sudden break up with a lover in December had quickly plummeted into full-fledged depression, complete with unwavering self-hatred. Since the lover had left in a fury of blame, and since I'd always half-believed I was ruined anyway, it was an easy transition. Everything around me seemed to reflect my state of mind; the naked limbs of trees shook against unrelenting cold. Walking to or from campus through a small patch of Northern Virginia's suburban woods, I would occasionally find a frozen animal—a stray cat, a crow—just off the path, and unashamedly compare it to myself. *Left to die. Alone.* I have a penchant for masochistic fantasies, and lack of sleep amplified my sour mood. I'd been sleeping ten hours a week for two months. It made normal thinking, normal conversation, difficult. I'd stopped making sense—couldn't carry on a decent conversation, and could barely maintain my daily obligations. I'd retreated from all of my friends except one: the artist. He was also trying to breathe through a break up, and also didn't sleep.

I jerked up, made some noise of frustration, and threw back the covers. Sighed, let the sigh fall into a soft weeping. Caught myself. Shook my head. Stood up. Swooned back down. Stood up again, and walked the few steps across my room to my computer. If I wasn't going to sleep, I might as well amuse myself.

There was an e-mail from the artist with a large attachment. The body read, simply, "Here's some photos. Call me when you get them." They were the possible photos for the next album cover. We'd been working on the second album long distance. He'd sent me music equipment so that I could turn my bathroom into my own studio. The songs were sad, sad, sad, and we felt they were really true. I put on my headphones and clicked on the latest version of "I've Been Down." He hadn't had a chance to add a drum track yet, and the piano chords hadn't been switched to synthesizer, or guitar, or run through reverb. My voice was raw, unfiltered, singing back to me: *Midnight in December never kept anyone warm, and I've waited for the sunlight like I've waited for you to see me. But you only see what you want.*

Bleary-eyed, I clicked open the files he sent, one by one, and stared at myself the way a child might at a mirror—fascinated, rapt. There was a series of pictures of me in an orange dress and angel wings that seemed to me unrecognizably beautiful. The light fell onto my face incandescently, blaring out any imperfections in my skin—making it glow. I looked utterly confident, though I knew the look was utterly affected. It was cold in the artist's studio that day. He'd brought a wardrobe comprised of clothing he'd bought—guessing my size—and clothes M. no longer wore. They were all too big or too small and he had to pin them back or aim the camera only at the parts of my body that the clothes fit correctly. The angel wings were my idea.

They were wooden, part of a prototype for a large sculpture he'd already sold. They were a little dusty, leaning against a large turquoise-and-black panel. I didn't know why I wanted them so badly. A part of me said *don't be ridiculous*, while another part said *you have to put them on*. When I told the artist I wanted to wear them, he explained that they might be too heavy and he had no way to attach them "authentically" to my body. Instead, he nailed them to the back of a white chair and I sat in it to give the illusion that the wings radiated from my body. He shone a large halogen lamp in my direction. I felt glorious.

"Perfect," he said behind the heavy, black camera. Goosebumps rose on my skin.

I clicked onto another picture. It was a close up of a woman's face and her face reflected in a mirror. She was caught slightly sideways, brushing mascara onto her lashes, her nose just a few inches from her reflection. The edges of the photograph cut out the top of her forehead, her ears and hairline—emphasizing the long lashes, the pouty mouth and slight chin. Emphasizing it twice, in fact, because of her reflection. It looked like a mascara ad. Something must have gotten mixed up: I didn't recognize the woman. I dialed the artist's number. It was 3 a.m. East Coast time, which meant 1 a.m. in New Mexico, but I knew he'd pick up.

"Hello," he said. His voice was deep, and always had in it the lilt of slight amusement.

"Hey, were you sleeping?" I asked to be polite, though I knew the answer. He led a vampire-like existence: sleeping all day and working all night in his studio. It had been the source of many fights between himself and M., and now with her gone he had nothing to stop him from becoming completely nocturnal. There was an echo behind his voice that placed him squarely in his large, concrete warehouse of a studio.

"Insomnia. And what are *you* doing up at this hour?"

"Deploring my existence."

"Heartbreak's a bitch, man," he said it with concern, the way someone might say *I hear you*. "Got yourself in a headlock again?"

"More like a Vulcan death grip."

"Geek reference. Nice. I used to watch that shit too . . ." He paused, "You alright, or are you gonna jump?"

"I don't think I could do much damage from this window."

"Good."

"No . . . I'm okay tonight, actually," and then to change the subject, "I got those pictures you sent."

"Hot, right?"

"Yeah, especially the one that's not me." I realize there's a thread of jealousy in my voice that I can't cut out.

"What are you talking about?"

"There's this one—JPEG 1328. I think it's somebody else."

"Hmmm . . . I got all those on my laptop. Hold on." I can imagine him walking through the huge room—like a sloppy, chaotic art auditorium—the way he might step into and out of the track lighting as he walks. "Who do you think it is?"

"I don't know . . . maybe M.? Maybe some model you were working with for a painting?" I can't stop from feeling anxious about this, though I don't understand why. He laughs a little on the other line.

"What's so funny?"

"Nothing," he says, entertained. I hear the clicking of a computer keyboard. "Okay, I found it."

"Who is it?"

"It's you."

"It's not me."

"Okay, you're right, it's my *other* muse."

I mean to laugh, but instead I say, "Oh." *His other muse.*

Why did this bother me? It didn't violate any contract of our friendship for him to take pictures of other women. His love with M. had never once bothered me—never once had in it the hint of threat. Yet, the thought of him following another woman around with a camera, watching her put on makeup, giving her clothing, even as a joke, made me feel deeply insecure. It pushed at an order—a structure like a card castle—that I had never before perceived. What was at stake? I couldn't name it. I didn't want to be with him, didn't want, even, to be loved by him, but—*my other muse,* he said, and my throat dropped into my stomach. I felt a falling sensation, a clawing on the walls of my dreaming self, as I—a heavy thing—slid down.

Sparks landed on his shoulders, the closed lids of his eyes. He felt their quick stings and then their extinguishment. He rose from his knees and walked down the long stairway in a somber ceremony of his own making. Along the road home, everything seemed to tremble: the pale houses, the long blades of grass, even the sun shook lightly in the sky. He tried to calm himself with deep breaths, but his lungs, too, trembled. *What if Aphrodite granted my wish? What if she didn't?* He began to walk faster, then faster, then broke into a run. When he returned home, he rushed directly into his bedroom, where Galatea lay on his bed, propped up stiffly on her feather pillows. Small streams of sweat ran down his face. He moved quickly to lie down with her, gave her a kiss on her perfect lips, as he'd done so many times before, but this time, they were warm.

He pressed her lips again, began to run his hands over her ivory limbs, which were soft, yielding. He kissed her left shoulder, the crook of her elbow, her palms, and her fingers folded softly around his cheek in response. He looked up into her blushing face, then kissed her soft lips again. She was alive. In wonder, he began to study her veins, the curvature of her fine muscles, her ribs. When he felt her ribs she flinched away, laughing—a laugh like a bell. He grabbed her by the wrist and pulled her close to him again, pressed his body against her virgin body, the clothes barely a layer between them.

"You'll be my bride," he told her, but she shook her head, not understanding his words. So, he explained patiently, the way a father might to his own child, "Before this moment, you didn't exist. You live only because I love you. You have no choice."

I was on the floor of my bedroom, crying from exhaustion, still drunk from the two bottles of champagne we'd downed at dinner. The dinner was supposed to be an olive branch. The artist and I had fought bitterly over the sound of the second album. I wanted real instruments, my voice in the raw. He wanted more dance tracks. I told him I thought he was slaughtering my voice; he said my voice was no good to begin with. In the middle of the fight, he'd told me he loved me, made promise after promise about the life we'd have together. And then the exchange of e-mails, voicemails, becoming more and more bitter, furious, inconsolable, until I refused to communicate with him at all. We hadn't talked for months when he called to tell me he'd be in D.C. for the opening of The National Museum of the American Indian. He'd been invited to the opening ceremonies, and was showing his work at a small gallery in Dupont Circle. He asked if I would meet him for dinner, for old time's sake.

The artist paced around my small room in his black Gucci suit, shaking his head.

"This is how you treat a bro?" he said, amazed.

"God, just go home! Leave me alone! Leave me the fuck alone!"

"You weren't even going to let me in, were you?" He continued his monologue, unaffected. "I mean, what's the problem? What's *your* problem. We're friends for six years. I pay to fly you all over the fucking country. I feed you dinner after dinner. I listen to every sad story about every guy you fuck, stay up night after night fixing your shitty vocals—I could have hired a *professional* singer—and you wouldn't even invite me into your house for a beer?"

Over dinner, he'd been his old self. We'd laughed and drank and drank, and talked about maybe trying a third album. But on the cab ride from D.C. to Virginia, he'd lunged at me suddenly, smashing his mouth to mine, grabbing at my thighs. I shoved him away, stunned. He eased back to stare out the window a while. Then he tried again, as if he didn't remember what had just happened. The highway rushed past us as we fought, silently, in the back seat—him pulling, me pushing away, the entire ride to my apartment. When we arrived, I jumped out of the cab and slammed the door shut, started for my door. He got out of the cab and walked around to pay the driver. I shouted at him to get back into the cab. The driver sped off. He followed me to the door, guilting me into opening it, promising not to try to kiss me again. But he kept after me, vacillating between aggression and vulnerability. If he'd wanted to force it, he could have—he was much stronger—but each time I'd push hard, he'd loosen his grip—float up to pace around the room and berate me for being an ungrateful girl.

"It's pretty fucking obvious you want more than a beer," I said, sitting up.

"So what?"

"So, I'm not in love with you!"

"I'm not asking you to be *right now*. You just need to calm the fuck down."

"I'm not going to calm down until you're gone. I've been as nice as I can. I mean, how many more times can you keep paying the cab drivers to leave!" I'd called three cabs in the hour he'd been there, and he'd sent them all away.

"Yeah, it's pretty rude of you to do that to me, but I'm not freaking out." And it was true: he was calmer than I'd ever seen him.

"I *don't want to kiss you*, and I have to work tomorrow. Please please please please please please leave me alone."

"So that's it?"

"What do you mean?"

"I tell you I'm in love with you for the past six years. I tell you that I want to marry you, move here for you, take care of you, and you tell me to leave you alone? That's pretty cold, D. Icy, even."

"But you're *not* in love with me."

"You don't know how I feel."

"You have some fucked up version of me in your head, and that's who you love."

"Thirty thousand dollars."

"What?"

"That's about how much I've spent on this project. Between the photographers, the equipment, the printing costs . . . all the clothes, the dinners, the plane tickets . . . shit, it's probably close to thirty-five thousand . . . not to mention M. Not to mention the end of our relationship."

"I didn't have anything to do with that."

"Would you stay with a man who was in love with another woman? Talked to her every other night? Spent thirty-five thousand dollars on her?"

"Are you saying I should love you for the amount of money you've spent on me?"

"No. I'm just saying, thirty-five thousand dollars and six years for one kiss . . . expensive kiss."

I sighed heavily into my hands. I felt split open, capable of anything. But the fact remained that however unconscious I liked to believe it was, I was complicit in our exchange. We had made an unspoken deal, and I'd broken my end of the bargain. I did owe him something. Not for the money, or dinners, or late-night calls, but for the beautiful, false image of myself. I'd let him carve me into the thing he loved, but refused to love him in return.

"Sometimes I think it would be easier if I just fucked you and sent you home," I told him. He lost his cool then, but only in his voice. It trembled as he told me what a *vicious* little girl I was. He went to his coat, splayed black on my bed, and pulled out a permanent black marker.

"I'm going to help you remember what a mean thing you just said to me." He walked over to the painting he'd given me when I'd moved away from Santa Fe: a bright collage of yellow and orange, one huge butterfly in the center, and text from a coyote narrative at the bottom. It hung over the end of my bed. He wrote in permanent marker across the center of it "fucked you and sent you home, '04." Then he left the room, grabbing his coat on the way out. I remembered the other painting downstairs—a portrait of my own face that he'd given to me as a birthday present the year before—and ran downstairs to protect it, but when I arrived at the bottom of the stairs, I found him in the dark kitchen, reaching into the refrigerator—the door light shining into his face. He didn't look up at me.

"I hope you don't mind. You didn't offer it to me, and since I came all this way . . ." he said, pulling a bottle from the fridge and twisting off the cap. "I called myself a cab." He looked over the dim kitchen counters as if they might illuminate. "I can't believe you. It's like you're not even you. This isn't how it was supposed to go down. This isn't how it was . . ." He trailed off, swaying a little in the fluorescent light, his shoulder-length black hair a wiry mess around his slender face. He adjusted his thick glasses, then looked over at me, standing in the dark hallway, unable to respond. "This isn't . . ." But he never finished the sentence. He shut the refrigerator, set the full bottle down on the counter, and walked past me to the front door, where he slipped out in silence. I stood there staring at the closed door like a ghost in the dark.

✳

His process shows through. He hasn't erased the dimensions of her mouth, the lines that cut through the center of her forehead to her chin, the space between her eyes, a grid of perpendicular lines, small crosses through the features of her face. The canvas shows through at the base of her neck, and here on her cheek, just below her left eye, or right eye, depending on whether you believe you are looking at her, or she is looking at you. And the black paint of her hair drips across her shoulders. One drop is circled here, in the bottom left corner, trembling on the edge of her collar bone.

I don't think she looks like me. The skin is pale, yes, but uneven with washes of gray and the mouth is too red and thin. I don't recognize the dark, glossless hair, or the eyes resolved into silence, rain colored, looking across a distance to which they can't imagine an end. I'm trying to remember how this all started—the smooth, long gestures of his fingers circled in smoke, or his dark hair edging his jaw. Night light, sometimes blue or red, but always dim and his laughter blooming in it. It's easy to mistake gratitude for love. It's easy to mistake obsession for love.

We embarrassed his fiancée once, at the restaurant with the red walls when we both kept laughing louder and louder as she became more and more silent. How many years have passed since then? I draw out that memory—sketch a line from the center of my chest to the center of his chest, across the table where fuchsia bursts of laughter hang above his head. His fingers press the edge of the table where two lines streak from him: one toward me and one toward her. I miss this part—my eyes are closed or lost.

In the memory, I laugh so hard the room blurs. The smells of heavy sauces waft from the plates of other tables, but I don't know how to paint this. Instead, I paint his fiancée's face, mute above the bread basket, canvas wearing through her shoulder, the tips of her fingers erased. Soon, the small crosses carved into her eyes will consume their blue irises, or mark two lines across the table, one for him and one for me. I don't draw a line between her and me. Instead, I write measurements next to the single yellow flower opening in its fragile vase at the center of the table, and the tea light flickering next to it.

From this perspective, I can never see my own face, just the back of my head swept up in a brown knot, my spine curving away from the vertical line it's supposed to follow, toward him, and a bare hand touching his elbow, lightly, like a wind or swallowed drink. I want to turn myself around, there, in the memory, so that I could know if my eyes had begun their change to the gray eyes in his painting. If the rain, now, coming down softly outside, is the same rain that came down that night as we stepped out of the restaurant onto the pavement—without ourselves—and both disappeared.

Tornado

My brother, my sister, and I are all digging in our garden with imaginary shovels, miming a harvest. It's mid-July and nothing in the garden is ripe but we like the taste of unripe things, so sometimes we pluck a baby green bean, a sliver of carrot, a green tomato. Along the edges of the garden there are weeds with tiny green fruit that we discovered we could eat when we ate them and none of us got sick. It's mild in flavor, tastes almost of nothing—so we call it *bread*. As in, *we need to harvest the bread*.

We are pretending to be farmers, like Dorothy. Soon the tornado will come and we'll hide in our play house, but for now we're pretending we don't know it will come. Mileah, our youngest sister, sits directly in the dirt, her yellow ochre skirt a mess over her tanned, chubby thighs—dirt coating her toes. She plucks the bread—one for her pocket and one for her mouth—not bothering to sweep away the wispy, dark curls from her face.

"Save some bread for us, Mileah," I tell her, gripping my invisible shovel upright, "you never know when we'll need it." Mileah nods dutifully, then continues exactly as before. Our game is interrupted by our mother's presence in the backyard. She's dressed in her brown Pancake Corner uniform, her hair in a long braid down the center of her back. She walks across our small stretch of grass to the edge of the garden.

"Okay kids, I'm off to work," she says, and our shovels vanish as we drift toward her, each of us waiting for our hug. Between hugs and kisses—the scent of gardenia and butter—she gives instructions:

"Danielle, there's a ham in the refrigerator already cooked and some frozen vegetables in the freezer," quick shoulder squeeze and a kiss on my forehead, "your Dad will be home soon from work," bending down to hug Mileah, "try to be quiet and just—" hug to Jasmine, "try to stay out of his way." She ends her speech with a loud kiss on Jasmine's cheek, then Mileah's.

"Bye, Mom." Our brother, Micah, lumbers forward and braces himself, though grins when she hugs him. She's the only one in the family who can touch him without warning—muss his thick, dark hair. When she releases him, he runs back to the garden and picks up his imaginary shovel again, laughing and twitching a little. Because he's bent over and not paying attention, a little string of drool falls from his mouth.

"Gross, Micah. Wipe up your drool," I tell him.

"Wipe your mouth, sweetie," our mother says a little louder, and he does.

Jasmine and I look at each other. She crinkles her nose at me. In summer, her skin goes heavenly gold and her spun-honey curls go blonde. She's built bird-thin and never says more than she can with her eyes—hazel with yellow rings. She points her eyes at the garden when our mother is out of sight. We all drift back.

Micah is the oldest—older than I am by two years, though autistic, so treated as younger in mind. None of us understands this, or even thinks to understand. Just as we don't understand why our father arrives home from work red eyed, covered in dust, and waits for one of us to cross him—give him a reason. We only understand when to keep still and when to scatter—all of us except Micah, who always understands too late.

We're all crouched down like rabbits in the garden, our brother pulling up too many carrots. Jasmine looks at me—*He's going to get mad.*

"Micah, Dad will get mad at us if you pull up too many carrots," I tell him.

"Dad's not here."

"He'll get mad when he gets home."

"So. I don't care."

"Micah, you don't want Dad to get mad at you. You shouldn't pull up any more carrots." But he starts ripping them out of the earth at a faster pace. I jump over to grab his hands and he stands up, fists raised over his head.

"You're not the boss of me! You're not the boss of me! You're not the boss!" His eyes are closed and he sways a little, spit gathering thick in his mouth.

"Tornado!" I yell, and he stops. Jasmine and Mileah jump to their feet and run toward the play house. "Hurry up, Micah, or the tornado will get us." I extend my hand and he takes it, squeezing too hard from excitement. We run to the graying playhouse together, crouching (one by one) through the hole in the busted door. Micah and I are too tall to stand up in it anymore, though Jasmine and Mileah are just the right height.

Our father built the miniature house years ago from lumber leftover from a construction site. He drew up blueprints, dug a foundation, and had us help him hammer the beams into place. I remember climbing a ladder to hand him shingles for the roof—his dark, curly hair and thick beard lit up in the sun. I remember him saying *thank you* in his kind voice, but can't remember how long it's been since I heard it, or when it begin to change.

He finished the house with a heart-shaped window in the front door. The window was kicked out the first week it went up, along with the lower half of the door, so we rarely bother opening it anymore. The house has one room that is just big enough for all four of us to sit in—one in each corner—our knees bent and feet meeting in the middle. We put our arms over each other's shoulders and hunch down. Outside, the sky is a hazy blue.

"It's starting to get wild out there," I say.

"Yeah!" Mileah says, "I'm scared. It's so windy!" But she's smiling.

"Did you pick enough bread?" Jasmine asks, and Mileah nods. She opens her sweaty fist to reveal a handful of little green breads and we all take one to eat. Then Jasmine reveals four green cherry tomatoes and we eat those as well. I have a small handful of slender green beans, and Micah has too many quill-thin, flesh-colored carrots. We wipe these off on our shirts and eat them—grit and all. We finish, smiling.

"The crops will be destroyed!" Micah shouts his part, grinning wide and grabbing his ears.

"We have to pick all the crops before the tornado gets them!" Mileah says, almost squealing. Already she's up on her thick little feet, running out through the doorway.

"Wait!" I say, running after her, but she knows not to wait. I crawl out of the house after her and stand up so that I can swoop her up like a baby. She wraps her arms around my neck, laughing.

"It's very dangerous now," I tell her, "you have to be very careful, or you'll get hurt. Stay close to me." I put her down and she grabs my hand. When I look up, Jasmine and Micah are already in the garden: Jasmine pretending to pull carrots and Micah actually pulling carrots. He's jerking them out of the ground gleefully—two entire rows already gone.

"Stop!" I scream and lunge at him. He's startled back against the cyclone fence with his fists up again, a pile of carrots like tiny limbs at his feet. I look at Jasmine. She closes her eyes.

"Uh-oh," Mileah says softly. Micah stares at the pile, too, as if he weren't the one who made it.

"Dad's gonna be real mad," he says finally.

"Pick them up," I tell him, and he gathers them up. "Maybe he won't notice," but I don't believe this. "Besides, the wind is getting stronger. We have to get to the cellar before the tornado comes."

We walk toward the playhouse and slump together in the little room. We scoot our feet back and Micah drops his pile of carrots in the center. We huddle around it.

"The tornado's getting closer," Jasmine says, cheerlessly.

Mileah says, "It's really close now."

"We're all gonna die," Micah says, his large, brown eyes wide, his lean face suddenly frail.

"Shhhhhh. We're not going to die. We're going to stay together," I say, and we pull our huddle in tighter. Mileah's little hand finds its way into mine. My heart beats faster. I look over Jasmine's bowed head through the broken slats of the door and out into the heat-stained sky, wondering what to do. We're quiet, listening for wind—trying to imagine a tornado coming through, sweeping us away, until we hear the exhausted engine of our father's red van pulling into the drive, and we all know how this game ends.

Still Life with Sparrow

Although it's small, we see first the brown wing twisted back and the little throat pulsing beneath its smooth feathers, one yellow eye shifting wildly. Tiny talons arch to find a stable thing in the air, but nothing. Scratching at nothing. On its back in the gravel alongside the highway. We are crouched down, our hands stretched out uncertain, leaning over the bird. Behind and up to the right, a twist of pine and scrub oak are still in the static summer air. The road expands deep into the trees, over the long hill ahead, seems to dissipate into the horizon. And beyond the horizon, the city we grew up in, where a boy I never met jumped into the Willamette, let the river water fill his lungs. His body drifted downstream for miles until someone found it snagged in a net. The boy crouching next to me knew it would happen this way. They were friends. The drowned boy came to him in a dream to tell him not to follow him there (where his body was) and kiss him goodbye. He tried not to think of this each night as he went to bed—tried to erase the face of the drowned boy on the bridge, walking backward into the mist of the dream saying, *It's the same here as it was in life, but everyone is a stranger.* A few yards down, the dirty blue van with its doors thrown open, a new crack of red in the windshield, and tent stakes and backpacks obscuring the faces of our companions, who have stopped asking *What is happening? Why did we stop?* The boy and I don't know each other well, but we know better than to think this death is a small thing. His smooth throat pulses like the bird's—thin blonde hair partly pressed against his forehead, partly feathered up in a mess. He smells of sweat, tobacco, cedar, some unidentifiable sweet. I'll know this scent the rest of my life, not as something physical, but something true. We are still while the bird shudders, slows, tries to flip over, blinks its thin eyelid, stops. The taillights of the van on the shoulder of the road blink red. Not even the wind speaks. Behind the hill, outside the frame, cars thrum on to distant cities. A thin sliver of moon betrays itself in the afternoon sky.

It's raining lightly. The rain pools into sections of gloss on the dim street as I stand at a corner, staring straight down the wide, busy street in front of me, then the long, darker, narrow street to my left, trying to remember where I am. My heart is pounding hard. An Asian couple walks by me, side by side beneath a single black umbrella. The man glances over his shoulder at me, looking confused—or maybe he is expressionless. Maybe the confusion is on my face. I have to remember what city I'm in. If I can remember the city, I can remember where I am in my life. This is the only thing I know right now, and I only know it intuitively. It switched on like an emergency generator when the rest of my mind's grid blacked out. The wide road thrums with traffic and I'm trying to glean clues from it. An Asian man on a motor scooter drives by, sloshing waves in the deep, muddy stream at the curb. Then another motor scooter drives by. This one has an entire Asian family on it: a man driving, a woman with short hair in a fitted silk tunic dress, riding sidesaddle on the back, holding a baby to her chest. She looks disinterestedly at me as she floats by, as if she already knows my name: it is a bore to her. Motor scooters. *Ao dai*—that's the kind of dress she was wearing—why do I know this?

I look at a break in the pavement, follow a delicate vine that loops up a metal pole, and at the top, a single yellow flower, twisted shut like an ancient eyelid, trembling out over the street sign: Thi Sach Street. *Ho Chi Minh City, Vietnam*. Suddenly I feel my hand gripping the hook of an umbrella, which is why I'm in shadow and not damp. My memory unravels like a scroll—creates a pinpoint *you are here* in the timeline of my life. I feel my toes crammed into the lovely purple heels I'm wearing, my stiff jeans holding in my flesh, the wind touching my face. No one emerges from the shadows to smother me. I begin the mental checklist: *My name is Danielle. I'm twenty-one and ported in Ho Chi Minh City for a few days while the ship is being repaired. We had a minor crash going up the Saigon River. Breathe. I'm meeting friends—I hope they will be friends—at a club. Joellen wouldn't come with me. My heart can stop pounding now, please. The Mekong Delta is flooding. The directions to the club are in my pocket.* I squeeze two fingers into the tight pockets of my jeans and pull out a strip of paper that says, "Apocalypse Now, 2C Thi Sach St." I vaguely remember paying a taxi driver (an old man with a motor scooter). I must have gone blank after he dropped me off. Reflexively, I look behind me. A lone man shuffles half a block away, his hands deep in the pockets of his khaki jacket, and behind him a glittery fistful of white girls, laughing wildly. The rain has become a fine mist, as if I'm standing in someone else's memory. I shut my umbrella and look at my watch, realize I'm early. I couldn't have been standing there long—two minutes, three minutes. *Where do I go when that happens? Nevermind. This is the street.* I see a neon glow a few buildings down and walk toward it, thinking of the flood.

When I find the building, I am unimpressed. Above the broad cement stairs and potted tropical plants, "Apocalypse Now" is written in an orange neon scribble inside a hot pink neon oval—as if the sign were written in fire and circled with lipstick. It was described to me as the hot spot for expatriates, tourists, prostitutes, and thieves. I agreed to go only because of the club's glib name. *How brash*, I thought, *what nerve*. I'd only seen the film in slices at a party, four years earlier—a Boot Camp Bash for a friend who had decided to enroll in the Air Force Academy instead of a regular college like the rest of us good, northwestern liberals. The decorations were glib: plastic water machine guns, crepe paper vines winding around the living room furniture, and a barrage of Vietnam War films, one after another, playing full volume on the big screen TV. Adam suggested red velvet cake (in the shape of a soldier) with camouflage icing, but no one wanted to make it. We were products of decades of Hollywood activism: going into the military meant killing, dying, and/or a lifetime of violent flashbacks. We believed we were doing the right thing—that if we reminded him of all the horror of war (albeit glam-horror), Matt might decide, last minute, to chose a life we understood. We pretended it was a joke, but Matt saw right through it. "Very funny," he said flatly when he walked into the room, "nice of my friends to support me." Everyone tried to cajole him into a better mood, but all through the night he was pensive and we were prematurely nostalgic for a friend we felt certain we would never see again. We all sipped our illegal beers slowly, peering down into the brown bottlenecks as if into the very heart of darkness.

My hair is beginning to fray in the humidity, so I go through the wide, stucco archway that leads to the dark main room of the club. Practically no one is there. A few people are clustered in small groups on the periphery of the room, murmuring over their gin and tonics, dressed for something scandalous. It's clear I'm not there with anyone. My heart sinks. I decide that, even though it's impossible anyone I know arrived before me, I will make it clear to the other patrons that I am looking for someone. *I have a friend. Lots of friends. A whole crowd will join me as soon as I find them.* I exaggerate my gestures of boredom—sighing, looking at my watch, shifting from foot to foot, looking toward the entrance, looking through the room with my hand above my eyes as if shielding from sunlight, realizing this doesn't make sense, and looking at my watch again. A Vietnamese woman dressed in a tight black cocktail dress clicks past me, balancing a tray of tropical drinks on her palm. She might be gorgeous or hideous—her face is a gray blur in this light. She disappears into another room, or a patio, I can't tell which, where someone might be waiting for me, so I follow her.

It's a patio, part of it covered by a series of pale stucco arches—architecture from a different era. The waitress delivers the drinks to three Vietnamese men on the patio, all boisterous in conversation. I listen to them talking—their intonations, the way they hit their consonants—without understanding a word. They say something quick and friendly to the waitress and she laughs politely. Tall, stocky palm plants splay out from their thick pots, lined like soldiers against the wall. Water drips lazily from the roof at the edge of the patio. I realize I am staring at the table, at a wedge of dragon fruit one of the men has taken off the lip of his glass and placed on a napkin.

Earlier in the day, I'd gone to a tropical fruit farm about an hour outside the city, just a few miles into the Mekong Delta, where the floods had drawn back enough. On the bus ride there, I'd read an article in broken English that described last week's flood as the worst in four decades. The body count was rising by the day—so far, 421 people had drowned, more than 300 of them children and infants. The floods were given some international attention, but a week had passed and like the tributaries, reporters had ebbed back into muddy obscurity. Vietnam has always endured the monsoon season as part of their geography, but cyclical floods had increased in severity and frequency since the Vietnam War—lingering effects of bombing and defoliation carried out by the United States. Agent Orange. The article didn't take this stance. It was short and flat, offered no blame. I watched mud make a patchwork of the landscape as the bus swerved at high speeds (right lane, left lane, it doesn't matter here)—water lilies blurring in the ditches along the road.

At the farm, I disappeared inside a small group of tourists: a few white-haired women; a few backpacked youth; a tall, barrel-chested white man in his sixties in a camouflage shirt—a veteran, I guess. We all have on the conical straw hats we purchased for a dollar each in the farm's main office. After a tour of the orchards, and a boat ride (two to each long, slender boat, each with a woman in an *ao dai* on the bow, paddling slowly through the maze of elephant grass that rose up all around us—the water so close to the lip of the boat if I dropped my hands to my side my wrists would be submerged. I imagined we looked like insects sitting in the creases of a procession of leaves, floating down the muddy body of Cửu Long), a fruit tasting. In an outdoor pavilion, we were given snake wine—good for men's virility, the guide told us—slices of mangos with salt and chili powder, and each a whole dragon fruit, which looked, not unconvincingly, like a waxy replica of a human heart.

"Dragon fruit," the guide told us as she dropped one on each of our paper plates, "or Love Fruit. Depends on who you ask." She was a small, stocky Vietnamese woman with a blunt haircut beneath her conical hat. She had wide-set eyes and a bright, frank manner. She'd given this tour a thousand times and liked to deviate from the script, tease the customers, alleviate her own boredom. "If Love Fruit, be careful how you slice it," she said, and we chuckled. "No, really," she said, smiling at her own joke, "tradition is that you give the largest piece to the one you love most. Whoever gets the second piece is probably angry." She gave each of us a plastic knife.

"What if we plan to eat the whole thing ourselves?" the veteran asked, sitting up proudly at his own conjecture. The guide lifted her chin so that he could see her eyes clearly as she considered this. She smirked, clasped her hands behind her back, tilted her head to the side.

"Then you are *selfish*," she said. Everyone laughed but her.

"Madam, do you want something to drink," the waitress in the black cocktail dress asks, a hand on her hip and a hand balancing the tray, like a caricature of a waitress. *Madam*. Does this means she thinks I'm older than she is? I look into her heart-shaped, not-quite-beautiful face, framed by night-rain and stucco arches. When she speaks, her front teeth stick out like round piano keys.

"Yes," I stammer. She stands there waiting for me to tell her my order. I only know I don't want a vodka tonic, but this is the only drink that comes to mind. What I want is a taste of that man's dragon fruit drink—a white, sugary wedge of dragon fruit settled in its red skin. I want to give the wedge to the guy I'm meeting here, or eat it all myself if he doesn't show up. She begins to look impatient. My heart pounds. Why is everything so hard to think through?

"Vodka and tonic, three limes," I say and she nods, swerves around me to the club's main room. I lean against a wall, trying to look casual. My feet already hurt. A techno beat thumps out of the main room and I walk over to glance through the doorway. Inside, the strobe lights and disco ball have begun their display, and a handful of scantily dressed white women—the girls from the street?—yelp and grind on the dance floor. Everyone else is seated, calm, pretending they're not interested. It reminds me of every middle school dance I ever attended—complete with sinking feeling and datelessness. The waitress emerges from the darkness like a magician with my drink. My drink. Yes, I need a drink. I pay her, and down the sharp, clear liquid through the tiny black straw in one suck. The waitress goes to check on the men, and by the time she returns to me, my glass is empty.

"You want another drink?" she asks. She doesn't seem to be judging, so I nod *yes*.

"You here alone?" This time she's judging.

"No . . . I mean, *yes*. I'm waiting for someone. For a group of someones. I'm waiting for a group of my friends."

"Those your friends?" She points toward the dance floor. I pretend to appraise the white girls for the first time.

"No. Doesn't look like it. I'm waiting for a couple of guys."

"Okay," she says as she disappears back into the darkness before I can read her face. I want to follow her, slink into one of those dark, corner tables, but I'm afraid she won't find me if I do and I need that other drink to have something to do with my hands, my mouth. *This time, drink it slowly. You don't want to be early-drunk. That's lame*, I admonish myself as I stare at one of the palm plants, until I realize that might make me look crazy, so I close my eyes. A door opens in my mind: a silhouette in the doorway.

I'm on a bed in a basement. Footsteps from the stairway have awoken me. I blink and someone is over me, barely distinguishable from the darkness. I say his name. I reach up to touch his face. He jerks away, grabs the edge of the sheets and yanks them back. I blink again and he's hovering over me, naked from the waist down—blink—my sight is obscured by his palm, pinning me to the bed by my face. *Shut up shut up shut up shut up*—I shake my head and open my eyes. A potted palm in dim light. The warm rain. I turn to find the waitress, nearly running into her as we arrive in the doorway at the same moment. She laughs at the almost collision.

"Here," she says, handing me the drink, "your friend here." I give her my fake smile, thinking she means my friend is booze. "Two guy walked in," she explains, "could be your friend."

"Oh, that's great! Thank you. Thanks a lot," I say slipping into the main room. It's busier now. A few couples have joined the white girls, trying to hold their drinks and each other and bounce rhythmically at the same time—they're making a mess of it. A lone man with curly blond hair keeps trying to join the group of dancing girls, but they only give him shoulders and backs, the universal sign for *you're not attractive enough*. I feel a hand on my shoulder and jump twelve feet, spilling the drink all over the floor. Johnny is looking at me intently, half-concerned, half-amused.

"Sorry. Didn't mean to ambush you," he smiles. It strikes me for the first time that he reminds me of a movie star, but I can't think of which one.

"Sorry," I say, reflexively.

"Why are you apologizing?"

"I don't really know. You're right. You should be apologizing to me." I try to say it flirty, confident, but it comes out defensive. There's a pause.

"I already did."

"Oh, right." Great. This is starting off great. We stand there for a minute with our stiff smiles before he offers to buy me another drink. I gratefully give him my order.

"Vodka and tonic, three limes." And he fades deep into the darkness of the room. Young Paul Newman, from *Cat on a Hot Tin Roof*. That's who he looks like: blue eyes, cleft chin, the whole bit. But I am no Liz Taylor. *Why is he even talking to me in the first place?* I recognize that this is probably the real source of attraction: we are a ridiculous, impossible match. He has a broad-shouldered build, steady eyes, and an ease with everyone—male and female—proof of a degree of confidence I can never even dream of having. I can't quite decide if I want to be *with him*, or want to *be him*—assured masculinity rising off my skin like cologne. *What would that feel like?* Absently, I take a deep breath in, then out, realizing how shallow I'd been breathing. Why are all my senses set to autopanic? I breathe in deeply again as Johnny approaches with my drink in one hand, a whiskey in the other.

"You okay?"

"I am now," I say, sipping from the rim of the glass before the exchange from his hands to mine is complete.

"Whoa. Slow down there, missy, or we'll have another spilled drink on our hands." He stands by me, observing the room. The crowd looks thicker, less clumsy and more purposefully riotous. I try to come up with something clever to say, but draw a blank. My heart pounds. *Jesus, calm the fuck down. You don't even know the guy. He could turn out to be completely lame.*

"Hey, where's Danny?" I suddenly find myself asking. Danny is never too far behind Johnny.

"Don't know. He was right behind me when I came in. Should we go find him?"

"Yes. He'll amuse us."

"I wasn't being amusing enough?"

"No. I want riotous laughter. You're not delivering." Danny is only mildly funny, but I'm trying to be a tough customer to increase my allure. I'm not sure what I'm trying to accomplish with this stance. Somewhere in a back room of my mind I imagine peeling back the thin cotton layer of his shirt, unbuttoning his jeans, but once he's exposed, I blank out—can't feel my own limbs or face—float into silence over our bodies like a helium balloon.

"Alrighty, let's see if we can find Danny boy," Johnny says, and I follow him as we weave through the now-crowded room, looking too closely into people's faces. The music is strong now, and it's difficult to hear. We find Danny on the patio, his hair gelled down and smile wide, talking to a group of guys—all loud frat types. They're quoting boot camp scenes from a movie—*Full Metal Jacket*?—and laughing like hyenas. I have no idea how they've wandered into the topic, or why it's funny. I try to look cognizant and amused. When I finish my drink, I excuse myself to get another. Johnny doesn't look in my direction when I leave.

The club's main hall is now full of drunk dancers. *I just can't do this right now*, I think. *I feel too fucked up*, but can't articulate why. *I should have stayed back at the ship.* I pay for and drink my third and fourth vodka tonics quickly and everything begins to feel warm, soft, a haze of effervescence over the room. Suddenly, I want to dance. I walk along the perimeter of the crowd, looking for a way in, and decide it's best to just go for it—everyone is huddled like penguins—barely able to move, but constantly moving. Strobe light, black light, glitter light from the disco ball, a song I almost recognize obfuscated into meaningless clips, driven over by hard rhythms. I'm deep in the crowd now—nearly at center. If I fall here I'll just fall into another body. I dance vertically, my hands above my head, jumping in place—this is all I have space for. My heart's pounding good and my head becomes a fuzzy, distant thing, separate from the sweat of my body. I close my eyes and jump harder—a weightlessness—I could almost float out of the room—and suddenly someone's hands are on my hips. I glance behind me: a dark-haired man I don't know. The dancer in front of me careens back and I'm thrust into the stranger—his damp, bony chest to my back. He slips a hand around my hips to my belly—a thumb just inside the belt of my jeans. When I try to push away from him he pulls me in tighter. My breath shortens, heart pounding bad and I freeze.

Silence rushes in. The music is a distant tapping—footsteps on basement stairs in a faraway city—my breath is not my breath, my body not my body. Dancers rise and fall around me, limbs flailing without regard to content or form—a recklessness of flesh. I feel sick. *I have to get out of here.* I say it out loud now, "I have to get out of here," but my voice disappears like exhaust in traffic. I elbow my way away from the guy, through the crowd, everyone tumbling into me. Someone grabs my shoulders and shakes me, hard. Darkness rushes over me. *I have to get out of here.* Someone flings their open palm into my face, stinging my cheek. I push harder now, without regard to civilized behavior. When I break free of the huddle, I rush through the crowded room, and out of the corner of my eye I see Johnny, leaning against a wall—talking close to a long-limbed brunette in a red dress. He laughs. I hesitate for a moment in the doorway that leads outside, then push through the doors, stamp onto the glistening pavement, breathing hard. A few men are smoking near the doorway.

"You need ride?" One of the men steps forward, stamping out his cigarette and gesturing toward a motor scooter. He's a young Vietnamese man in a loose green T-shirt and khaki shorts. We're the same height. I swallow, trying to catch my breath.

"How much?"

"Where you go?"

"The Hotel Continental," where the ship and my room are just a short walk away. We agree on a price and he boards the bike. I swing a leg over the back and slip forward—my thighs tight around his hips. *Don't panic. It's fine. It's fine.* I lean to grab the back of the seat, tears welling up. *Goddamnit. Don't fucking start now.* If I didn't need both hands to hold on, I'd slap myself across the face. Instead, I squeeze my fingers so tight around the edge of the seat I can feel them burning. My knuckles are white meteors streaming through the darkness as he pulls quickly away from the curb where water rushes and rushes, down the street, into the wide avenue, following us in and out of alleys—we can't lose the water, even when he turns sharply to the right, to the left, weaving in and out of traffic—the water only accumulates, tumbling after us, swelling like disdain—like a secret that nobody keeps.

Finally, we reach the hotel. I pay him and begin walking immediately away, following the pace of my heart, until I find a narrow alley to hide in, and cover my burning face. Full panic hits. I'm hyperventilating. *Fuck. What's wrong with me? What's wrong with me?* The street shines slick as a knife. I close my eyes. I'm fifteen, stumbling through a neighborhood in Spokane, Washington. It's 2 a.m., 3 a.m.—I'm not sure what time it is. I just know I need to get out of here. My hips don't work quite right and the blood is still sticky between my thighs. I can't feel my legs, so I'm telling them what to do. *Keep walking.* Portland, Oregon, is a six hour car ride away, but I think maybe if I start walking now—I just need to know the direction—the direction—all of the houses are the same sleeping face. I don't have a map or money. I wasn't thinking when I left. The scene keeps coming back to me as I flash beneath the streetlights: long bars of light from the lone window stretch across the basement room as if encaging everything. My cheek presses against the ceiling. The ceiling. Funny to be floating here, above the scene. Below, I can hear my breath being slammed out of me, my head hitting the wall, over and over. Darkness so complete, it's almost lovely—pouring into me like a swift, deep current. When I turn around I see my own body below (*you see yourself below, shaking*) as he withdraws to the edge of the bed, dresses slowly, and disappears through the door. My body is splayed and frozen in the center of the naked mattress—a dark form in a river of darkness. I go back to my body.

Where are we now?

I wake late, my joints a little swollen, my eyes light-sensitive—a terrible headache. The body has a memory. When I walk up to the main deck, I sit there a long time, my mind becoming part of the landscape: autumn-thick currents and trees rising like apparitions from the mud-dark water. Band of river. Band of jungle. Band of watery sky. The city blurred behind a thicket of rain. This river is in the center of Cửu Long, "Nine Dragons"—a name describing the nine branches of the delta system that sprawls over the jungle landscape and empties into the China Sea. Auspicious number nine is kept in the name, though two of the branches silted over years ago. Two dragons, drowned.

The repairs to the side of the ship are nearly finished. All week, workers have been welding—sparks diving into the water. The pilot hired to navigate us safely through the perils of the Saigon Port crashed us into a barge on the way to our pier. The safety drills we'd been running periodically since we boarded suddenly took on real meaning as we lined up along the rails in our orange life jackets, waiting for the word to board the emergency boats: women and children first. *Thank god I'm a woman*, I thought as I stood there, shoulder to shoulder with my shipmates, realizing I'd never had the thought before. It was the only context I could think of in which my gender might save me. But we never got to the boats. The damage was fairly minor, which is to say, the hull wasn't broken. The barge-shaped gauge in the side of the ship spanned several decks, but all above the water line. In only a week, the ship has been stitched back together with fire and we'll be leaving soon.

I don't know how to feel. Instead, I watch the men on other boats, working their hands, brown as the river, into and out of the ropes along the pier, the holds along the ships. They grasp oars, nets, and dip them into or pull them from the water, attenuate the water, and meanwhile the rain, wetting their shirts, dripping from the edges of their conical hats, doesn't dim the daylight—the rain falling like light itself, and the tamarisks and bamboo, heavy with light, bow to the bodies floating in the river, way downstream, bow to the swollen limbs and faces—the pearly cast of their skin—

"Good morning, sunrise," Joellen's cheery voice breaks through my meditation, "was Apocalypse Now as fun as the movie?" Jo is lovely and blonde with a long, elegant face, sharp chin, and large aqua eyes. She finds it amusing to tease me when I'm in a bad mood.

"It was *just like* the movie, actually."

"Yeah? Did you take a river tour with a machine gun? And more importantly, did you find the colonel?"

"That's such a good movie," Corey says, moving into my line of sight.

He has on his Vietnamese flag T-shirt—all red with a yellow star on his chest—and stands with both hands on his hips. He's short and compact with a shaved head and muscular shoulders that at this moment are thrust back. Overall, it gives him the appearance of a minor superhero.

"I don't know what you're talking about," I admit.

"Good. It's better that you're confused. Makes you more susceptible to suggestion," Joellen says conspiratorially.

"And what are you suggesting?"

"That you should come with us," Corey says. As if on cue, the rain suddenly lets up.

My plan was to sit here all morning—try to untangle my memories, put them into neat glass jars—try to understand why they keep floating up like once-buried shrapnel. *Why here? Why now?* But I'm sick of being alone. I'm sick of my own mind. I agree to go.

"Great. Here's your stuff," Joellen says, producing my backpack. She'd be the Girl Scout type if Girl Scouts were funny and liked cheap beer.

"How did you get that?"

"When we went down to your room. Your roommate was still there."

"And she just gave you my stuff?"

"Pretty much," she says, standing. By the time we leave the ship, my mind's changing to better weather—little blue patches dissolving clouds. We decide to hire cyclos to take us to the Ben Thanh Market because it's in Corey's travel guide.

This part of the city is low, still ankle-deep in water. A bare-chested man stands in the flooded market selling coconuts. I give him a dollar and he severs a brown tip with his machete, pushes a straw through for me to drink. I try to tell him *thank you* in Vietnamese, but can't make the sounds right on my tongue. He looks confused.

"Is that safe to drink?" Jo asks, inspecting my coconut. The captain has warned us about tuberculosis, malaria, diphtheria, hepatitis, and something bacterial called *black hairy tongue.*

"Probably not," I say, sipping my drink.

"So, you just have a thing for tropical diseases?"

"Yeah." I use my best devil-may-care voice.

"Makes me wish I was a tropical disease," Corey says, smiling. I'd made the mistake of kissing him the first night we met, before I realized we had very little in common and he had a penchant for bad jokes.

"You *are* a tropical disease," I say.

"Okay kids," Joellen moderates, "let's be civilized." After all, he's the reason that Joellen and I met. He and I were standing in line, bickering about something, when he told me he didn't like me so much right now and that he'd rather talk to anyone else.

"Good. Fine with me. Talk to someone else," I said. Corey turned around to the girl in front of us and tapped her on the shoulder—asked her where she was from.

"Nazareth," she answered instantly, clearly aware of the implications. I liked her already.

"Oh, really?" I cut in, "Is that anywhere near Bethlehem?"

"Actually, yes," she said.

"Are you Jewish?" Corey asked, seriously.

"Pennsylvania Dutch. Unaffiliated," she answered. Later, we learned she meant Nazareth, Pennsylvania.

"And your name?" I had to know.

"Joellen." Jo.

The three of us had learned our traveling pattern together. Corey and I would bicker and get us lost, and Joellen always found our way back. She didn't seem to mind the work—seemed almost to like it. There wasn't much to make us stick except a collective delight in the absurd and that our little group was the closest thing to having a history with anyone on the ship.

"We'll be good," I sing, then take another sip of my coconut and turn back to the market.

Beneath the tin roof—a patchwork of nails and rust—there are dresses, hats, fruit, fried noodles, naked flanks of meat, jewelry, shoes, air-brushed art, incense, herbs, pottery, wooden sculptures. I get lost in the cornucopia and drift away from Jo and Corey—find myself in front of a seafood stand, half-live fish staring from crates filled with ice. Their scales gleam and sometimes one lifts a tail as if it might suddenly swim away. The body has a memory.

Across the aisle, a few booths down, my eyes land on an old Vietnamese woman in a lavender dress. She's sitting in a folding chair, plucking the limp body of a goose. Slowly. She's so slow there's something deliberate about the slowness; her gaze is the size of each feather. She looks sad. I wonder if she's lost someone in the flood—her plucking a kind of vigil. But there's something else about her I can't quite place—something familiar. *There's no way I know her*, I reason.

It has something to do with her expression. It says, *the floods, the war, the French, the war again, the Americans, the war again, my children, the ruined water, the torn fields, the floods again.* I wonder if anyone can live with that much. *Not all the time*, I decide. *No one can live with that much trauma all the time.*

The Vietnamese have a smiling culture—a smile with ghosts beneath the surface. No one has treated me unkindly since I arrived, though I feel they should. Maybe they've learned to forget. Maybe they live with a history of forgetting, then remembering, then forgetting again. It's as if the entire country, the land itself, suffers from posttraumatic stress. *I had to go back.*

I had no choice. I wandered around Spokane for what seemed like hours, until I found the house again. I had no money, no map, and no way of defining what had happened. I went back to the house, to the basement, and stripped off the sheets, brought them to the laundry room to wash out the blood, so no one would know. I remember wondering who to blame as I twisted my hands in the sheets in the dim basement. He was my boyfriend—I'd let him kiss me before. I'd lain down with him once on his parents' couch and let him touch me beneath my clothes. I was supposed to want this. Was I supposed to want this? Was it not enough to say no? I

wrung the sheets out as best I could, laid them down on the bed, and fell
into an anxious, desperate sleep.

The drive back to Portland was long and flat. We were mostly silent except the few times he felt moved to explain my failings—*stupid, virgin, slut*.
It was only June, but the grass along the highway was high and stripped of
color—almost gray, like rainclouds. And because the sky was overcast, it
looked like clouds over clouds. With each mile, I sunk deeper into myself,
trying to find a place to hide—to dismantle the memory and seal it away.

"Where are you, D?" Joellen's voice breaks through.

"What?" I heard her. I'm just buying time, trying to shake myself
present.

"I saw you all the way from the last booth. You've been staring at that
woman forever."

"Oh, yeah. I didn't even see her. I'm just spacing out. Must still be a
little hungover . . . and besides *you* were obviously staring at *me*."

"True. Kind of makes me wonder who was staring at *me*," she says.

"I was staring at both of you," Corey emerges with a wooden drum and
box of incense.

I call them both voyeurs.

"I'm bored of this place. Let's go somewhere else," Corey says.

"Ever to confess you're bored means you have no Inner Resources." I
quote Berryman, knowing he won't get it. He ignores it altogether.

"Let's find the tallest building in Saigon and go to the top of it."

"It's called Ho Chi Minh City now," Joellen corrects.

"Whatever."

"Okay, which building?" I have a dare in my voice. He marches out of
the aisle toward the street, stands on the corner with a wide stance, one
hand on his hip and the other shielding his eyes. At any minute, I expect
his T-shirt to grow a red cape. At the end of the block there's a bus full of
people—rooster cages with roosters inside them strapped to the bus roof.
Its wheels spin in the muddy water without gripping the pavement. There's
a crowd of people next to it, waiting for the next bus, their hands and eyes

nervous with the tickets they fold and unfold as if they hold the names of the ones they have lost and how to touch them again.

"There!" Corey sounds determined. "Follow me, ladies." And we do. We cross the wide street the way we've learned to: keeping an even pace while the traffic—mostly motorcycles and scooters, rickshaws, a bus here or there, riding without order on either side of the street—swerves around us—three little rolling stones in a river of traffic. When we reach the other side, Corey's stride picks up and Joellen and I keep pace just a little behind him, mimicking his walk. When this loses its amusement, we ask him to slow down.

"*Life* doesn't slow down, and we're chasing *life*," he tells us. I don't know where he gets these little sayings. Coaches? Gift cards? Motivational calendars?

"You're chasing a building," Joellen says.

"And gaining on it!" Corey retorts. We laugh together and pick up our pace. There's a lot of foot traffic on this street and we weave through the people at a near run.

"Why are we going so fast?" I ask, without wanting to slow down. We must look crazy.

"I don't know," Corey informs us, "but it's kind of fun, right?" Right. We move in our fast strut for about ten blocks, until the city begins to look familiar.

"You're leading us back to the ship," Jo announces. She has a startlingly accurate internal compass. I've been down this street before. We come to a corner that has a betel nut tree on the right and currency exchange office to the left. Beneath the tree is a beggar I recognize from a few days ago.

I was walking aimlessly, in and out of shops, not buying anything. For blocks, I was followed by a beggar on a makeshift skateboard, smiling as he held out his mangled hands, sometimes gesturing toward the scarred, twisted flesh that might have once been his legs, or maybe (his face was young) he was born that way—a little Agent Orange in the river? I'd given him money three times, but he still rolled behind me, smiling and holding out his hand each time I looked even vaguely in his direction. Finally, he followed me into a shop. Nothing about this was funny, but the shop-keeper and I smiled at one another when I stepped into her boutique to escape him, and again when he followed me in, his bright face almost lost in the jungle of women's wear. After a while, she half-heartedly gestured the beggar away. She spoke to him gently and he left without a word. She nodded to me as if to say *okay, I did my part*, but her smile was gone. I wanted to buy one of her silk dresses, but when I reached into my pockets—I must have given it all to the beggar—I didn't have anything left.

I don't look at the beggar as we pass him, though in my periphery, I think I see him raise his hand. I feel his twisted hand inside my head, moving things around. *Just keep walking. Look straight ahead. Don't think about it.*

"You're not taking us back to the ship, right? You have a plan, Corey—right?" Jo says, a little out of breath.

"Exercise is good for you!"

"Yes, we know that, Corey," I say, also out of breath, "What we want to know is if you have a *plan*."

"See that dirty-white awning?" He points to a spot about half a block away.

"That's it?"

"That's it."

The building itself is huge, sleek, and black. The seams are black and the wall-sized windows are all tinted black. When I crane my head back, I see the shorter buildings reflected in it, warped a little out of shape. We go right up to the revolving doors (black glass) and walk in. The lobby is empty, but impressive: cathedral-like ceilings, marble floors, and a glossy walnut-colored desk the size of a car where two men in dark suits officially sit. We pause a bit in the center of the room, unsure of what to do. One of the men behind the desk tells us something in Vietnamese.

"Hi," Corey says, "we don't speak Vietnamese." Jo and I wave hello, smile. Just then, Corey sees the elevators and we go straight to them.

"Only twenty-three floors," Jo says. "This can't be the tallest building."

"We're here, though."

I chime in: "Let's just go to the top to see what we can see." All agree. We board the first available *up*. Corey presses floor 23. A man's voice, filled with static, comes over the elevator speakers—some kind of instructions?

"We don't know what you're saying," Joellen says to the elevator ceiling where the voice seems to come through. The elevator stops at floor 21 and the doors threaten to open.

"What? No way, man, we're going to the top!" Corey hits the *door shut* symbol and compulsively presses floor 23 like an arcade button. We're going up again, laughing at nothing. The voice blares through the speakers again. This time, it sounds urgent—or stern? Or excited?

"We're sorry, but we don't understand you!" I tell the voice, raising my shoulders in an exaggerated shrug in case there are cameras. We all think this is hilarious.

"We don't understand you! We don't understand you!" The three of us chant, overlapping each other—a hysterical fugue of misunderstanding. But when the brassy doors open and we step out onto floor 23, we stop laughing. It's clear we're not supposed to be here.

The entire floor—as tall and wide as an auditorium—is gutted: no divisions into rooms, just concrete, structural beams, and walls made of tinted glass. There's nothing to obscure our view of the cityscape, and it's stunning.

"Whoa!" Corey runs swiftly across the huge room and smashes his face to the glass. Jo and I look at each other, trying to decide whether we should also smash our faces against the glass, or return to the first floor like good citizens.

"I don't think it's illegal . . . the worst they could do is ask us to leave, right?" I venture.

"And no one has come for us yet," she agrees.

I skip over to the window-walls. Jo gallops. We swoon over the scene. To the right and left there's the city below in miniature: the cars, cyclos, people moving in the loose pattern that the streets define, and around them the pastel buildings, and around the buildings the jungle curling around poles and phone lines, palms and betel nut trees bursting through pavement. And in front of us, everything is green-wild and water. The river snakes out, glistening and lovely. Beyond it, water flattens the landscape into a muddy delta. From this distance, everything is lovely. I can see how the river might flood the city—not to tear down what people build, but to take itself back—how the river is the memory of the land.

We hear the elevator *ding* behind us, and when the doors open we see three Vietnamese men in casual street clothes—T-shirts, sneakers, baggy shorts, one with a backward cap—all carrying automatic rifles. Behind them stands one of the men from the lobby, beautifully clean and calm in his navy suit, his hands clasped behind his back. The men hold their guns exactly the way army men carry guns in movies when they are stalking an enemy. They move low in the hips, approach us slowly, assessing the situation. Their hands are certain, but faces confused.

The three of us look at each other, the men, each other, and finally decide to raise our hands above our heads—*this is the way we surrender, right?* The man in the suit speaks to the men with the guns and the men answer uncertainly, their vowels wavering, their consonants clipped. They lower the points of their guns, clasp them across their chests, and for a moment everyone is quiet.

Finally, one of the automatic rifle men—the man with the backward cap—speaks to us, and though we don't know the language, we understand him: It's time to leave. He gestures toward the elevator and we obey. The man in the suit stays behind, so that it's three guns and six people standing together in the narrow shaft, our elbows touching as we stare up at the curved half-moon of the floor dial. None of us dares to speak. Each floor number illuminates as we drift to the ground, as silent and as vulnerable as rain.

Blood clots like stars. Stars like courtesans. Mouth bruised from kissing. The humid vellum of summer air. In the new field, rows of soft earth and the seeds we disturb with the weight of our bodies. Half eclipse. My little sister steals my diary, asks if it hurts. Our father smashes the coffee table into splinters. I sleep in a slanted room and shake all through December. We listen to The Dandy Warhols. The bus is late. Boys whose names we say like psalms. Lake water scent of mud and rinsed fish. I begin to dream of the apocalypse. None of the fathers want anything to do with their children. No money for a dress for the dance. Pine needles stick through my sweater. His eyes are hazel and the most beautiful in the city. We take off our clothes and wade in. We listen to Super Deluxe. My little sister runs away with the boy down the block. Our father snaps the remote control in half. Richard says he plans to rape me. The weathermen talk of northern fronts and high pressure. The freeways arch up over the river, over the dim lights of sleeping buildings, and we're speeding over them, rushing music, his pretty mouth and right hand tense on my thigh. Stars like sisters. Sisters like trees on a faraway island. I have a cousin whose body grows slighter and slighter. He shifts down and we speed up. It was dangerous, but we wanted to anyway. Pile of wet leaves, the veins pressed together. Richard says he'll put a bag over my head so he won't have to see my ugly face while he does it and it'll hurt and he'll like that and he hopes that I'll cry; he'd like to hear me cry. The Willamette River floods again and school is cancelled. We listen to Pink Floyd with the lights out. A drive to someone's parents' cabin. Men with wedding rings and white sedans pull over to ask how much money I want to get into their cars. Monica shows up with an eyebrow ring and an addiction to anything that makes her go fast. My mother finds the box of condoms I keep beneath my bed. Waiting for the bus. Drinking stolen blush wine, watching *The Basketball Diaries*, Katie and I fall out of love with Leonardo DiCaprio. On the Fourth of July, he doesn't let go of the M-80 in time and breaks his arm in the blast. My mother wakes me, asks where my sister is. Until my cousin's arms were as thin as her hair, until the bones beneath her face. For the first time, I see myself naked because the boy I love has seen me naked and I want to know myself as he knows me. We get lost on the way to Lost Lake, and shiver all night as the tent trembles with rain. Smoke full of musk. Musk full of bodies. The airplanes that never take us anywhere. We listen to The Beatle's *Revolver* on repeat, high, uncertain of how long we've been kissing. Lace, taffeta, feathers—it doesn't matter because we can't afford a dress for the dance. Emma and I stay up, singing in rounds, sleeping as me and my sister once did. Brice breaks up with my sister when she becomes pregnant. Our father, still downing his vodka, throws his boot across the room. Instead of sleeping, I paint landscapes of open fields and skies I've never seen, dusty instruments, women asleep as they fall through the sky. Kissing among the mosquitoes. Kissing with my back against the steering wheel. I decide I want to be Catholic. Somehow my body is contaminated. Katie laughs her big laugh and I laugh my big laugh and we just can't stop laughing. List of songs for the mixed tape I'll make him. List of places I want to go. List of reasons to run away. My father finally leaves a week before Christmas, saying, "You don't know how good you have it now. You'll get so hungry you'll beg me to come home." We listen to Muddy Waters, imagining an ancient and brutal Mississippi. Emma and I start charting the moon—we're looking for answers. Light as a feather, stiff as a board. I dream a line of dark tornados on my street, sit down on my bed and wait to die. Whenever I walk through the neighborhood, I carry a sharp stick in my hand, just in case I run into Richard. Her water doesn't break, so at his birth, my nephew pushes out with the caul across his face. Somehow my skin is sulfur, pitch, naphtha, quicklime and I want another body to ignite me, burn me clean. My cousin becomes so slight, she can't speak—her voice on some other frequency. Monica and I sneak out of her window to meet Jim at the playground but he's late and her father has followed us and Jesus Christ is he mad. Amy stops fighting and starts smoking opium. We listen to Nirvana, jumping around like maniacs. I don't bother to sweep away the confusion of dark hair across my face. I learn that it's not okay to say the right answer; it is only okay to say the wrong answer. No one white is ever arrested on the evening news. I dream that I sacrifice my body and drift up into the gray, wrecked sky. "I love you so fucking much," my lover says, "I fucking love you." Kissing until the windows are opaque with breath. Fireworks dying as they fall. Waiting for the bus again. Mom gets a job at the grocery store, arrives home each night around 1 a.m. and floats on her own exhaustion into the corner of the couch. We are hungry, but don't beg him to return, don't even ask him, don't even call to tell him we're fine. Rhododendrons are sticky in spring, cling to our hair, the backs of our knees. We listen to Makeup, which used to be The Nation of Ulysses, which used to be Cupid Car Club. Mom stays up by the blue curtains, pacing the room, shaking her head. When I tell Kari Joy I've lost my virginity, she cries into her palms, says, *"How could you do this without me?"* Under the corner willows and streetlights, Alison smokes her Camels. Vespers and hymns. I learn how to hold a rosary with my thumb over a round prayer.

We follow the trail through unripe gooseberries and scrub brush straight to the top of Neahkahnie Mountain, look out over the Pacific, and I know that I love him but he doesn't love me. *Somehow*, I feel, the riots are my fault. I take the shapes in—let them become part of my body. Emma and I stay up late, holding hands and singing rounds. Richard disappears from school and for years I don't see him, but still think of him, of what he said. When I stay over at Amy's she doesn't want me to sleep so I pretend to sleep and she stays awake, leaning over me. Always waiting for the bus. I'm crowned homecoming queen. I don't tell my mom because what's the point? Myrrh and frankincense and Ecclesiastes. I learn how to fight, how to know when a fight is coming. We listen to U2. Purple thistles hide in the long, slender bodies of sweetgrass. In front of the whole church, I'm baptized, but feel nothing. I learn how to say *fuck you* without a wince of conscience. Katie and I feast on mangoes. After the dance, he takes me to the rose garden, but is too shy to try anything. The stink of sweat and uncertainty. My sister and I stop speaking, are suspicious of our new bodies, suspicious of one another. I stand there in my borrowed dress. So slight she can no longer hold the fluids of her body and begins to vomit bile. The bus goes by without stopping. I dream I awake naked in the neighbor's brambles. Rain warms on the hoods of cars. I don't want to kiss Amy, but I'm certain she wants to kiss me, and I'd probably let her if she wanted, but I'm certain she thinks that she doesn't. Someone touches my shoulder, and when I turn around to Richard's face I flinch back, my breath thrown, but he takes a step away, raises his hand, says he's found Jesus and "You were always a nice girl and didn't deserve what I said. I just want to say I'm sorry." My father shows up on the porch after he's smashed the headlights of Mom's car. In the kitchen, my lover can't articulate why he no longer loves me and I keep crying and throwing dry dishrags at his face. My cousin begins by sipping broth, then swallowing spoonfuls of rice; one day, she eats an apple. No money for presents, but I insist on a tree. Trees, like dark angels in the park at night, hover over us as he takes off his shirt. List of phone numbers. List of people I wish would die. We watch the multicolored lights flash and disappear in the thirsty pine. I hear he's kissing someone else now, a cheerleader. I sleep with a kitchen knife beneath my bed, just in case. "It's beautiful," Mom says after a long while. "I tried," I say. She says, "Me, too." I slip an arm out of the blankets and feel around the floor for an extra pillow. When I touch the edge of something soft, I pull it beneath, hold it tightly to my chest.

"Faint me," Monica says from the pillow side of her bed. I'm staying the night like I do every Saturday and we've fallen into a comfortable routine of radio, potato chips, talking about the boys who won't dance with us at our middle school semiformals and, as of a few months ago, fainting.

"No."

"I'll faint you back," she whines.

"No, I don't want to faint you and I don't want you to faint me. It freaks me out."

"I *promise* not to seizure."

"You can't promise that—you're not awake when it happens."

"Pleeeease. You haven't fainted me in *so* long. I tried to get Rachel to do it, but she's not strong enough." I almost laugh, imagining Monica's scrawny little sister standing on the couch with her hands around Monica's neck.

"If you really love me, you'll faint me," she continues, half-smiling, half-serious. She's cocked her slender, freckled face to one side so that her reddish hair falls straight down over her skinny shoulders. She's sitting with her legs crossed and leans forward onto her blue sheets, breaking some of the chips we've left there. Somewhere in the back of my mind the word *blackmail* rouses from its sleep, then turns over.

"Okay. But just once," I say. I'm a sucker, and we both know it.

"And then I'll faint you."

"Maybe. We'll see if I feel like it after you get done flipping out all over the place."

The truth is, fainting scares me. I don't seizure or have bad visions like Monica, but she's not strong enough to hold my weight, and usually has to tumble me down somewhere. The next day, I always find garish bruises for which I can't identify the source—a bump on my head, a purple elbow, a sprained foot, without any memory of original pain.

Monica stands up on the end of the bed.

"Just stand on the floor, Mon. It's easier to catch you that way."

"But falling's the best part. I want to fall *really long, really far*."

"Yeah, I know, but I'm afraid you'll get hurt."

"You'll catch me. I trust you."

"Fine." I pull a chair to the end of the bed so that she and I stand at the same height, facing each other. The mess of books, old cereal bowls, and dirty clothes makes a dizzying pattern on the floor. I swoon a little.

"Ready?" she asks. I hold my hands out in front of me, just before her neck, and plant my feet deeper into the chair.

"Yes. Go."

She folds over so that her head dangles between her legs and breathes as if she's hyperventilating—sharp, deep, quick—then shoots back to standing, holding her breath. I grab her neck, making sure to press my palms deep into both sides until I can feel her pulse struggling to get through her jugular. I start counting slowly—*one, two, three, four, five, six*—her eyes gloss, flicker closed—*seven, eight, nine*—her knees buckle and I push her slightly back, then leap onto the bed to catch her. Her long pale limbs slump down as I try—as gently as possible—to lay her on the bed. I lay myself along the edge to make sure she doesn't roll off. Her shoulder trembles a little against my shoulder and her mouth is ecstatically slack.

She moans, rocking her head from side to side. She lifts up her arms and lets them drop to her side, begins to hum. After a few minutes, she rolls over to face me and places her hand on my cheek, the haze cleared from her eyes.

"How was it?"

"Pretty good. Alright."

"Just alright?"

"I mean, yeah—it was good, I just wanted it to last longer. Will you do it again?"

"No."

"You just have to hold my neck a little longer is all."

"No. I said I'd do it once. Let's see if there's something on TV."

"Yeah, but you didn't *really* faint me. You didn't faint me good. You did it kind of chickenshit, like you were afraid to make me go deep."

"It looked pretty good from my perspective. You couldn't have said your own name."

"Yeah, okay, it was *pretty good*—it just wasn't long enough. Please? Just once more?"

"Just once, and then we'll see if there are any movies on."

"You *do* love me."

"Shut up."

We take our positions again and she drops down to breathe. When she stands she inhales extra deep and holds her breath. I'm a little angry as I press my palms into her neck—pale and skinny as a goose's—*she's always talking me into shit I hate doing. That time we snuck out of the house to meet those high school boys—what were their names?—and got lost and caught and those boys never talked to us again. And it's not as bad for her. Her dad yells and she gets grounded. But my dad—it's always worse for me. Why do I let her?* I watch the red rise in her face, an unconscious fog rolling into her eyes—realize I've forgotten to count.

Where are we now? Five? Six? Her knees buckle a little, but she manages to stay standing, so I keep pressing. Her eyelids half close, but don't shut—

a trance obscuring her expression. *How long is long enough?* I keep waiting for her to drop, but she only slumps, her pulse hard at the bottom of her neck, only a weak flutter at the top. *Sixteen? Seventeen?* Her shoulders start to tremble a little, then her hands twitch up so that she hits my stomach. I realize she's starting to seizure and let her go—try to grab her before she falls, but she shakes so violently, I can't get a grip and her long limbs flop everywhere. She bangs her elbows and knees against mine—hits her head against the wall, leaving a small dent—tremors lightly on the bed until she goes totally out, drooling.

"No roughhousing down there!" Monica's mother's disembodied voice calls from the top of the stairs at the front of the house. I jump down from the bed, open the door and yell, "Sorry," then go quickly to Monica to try and wake her—lightly slapping her shoulders, her face. She doesn't stir, so I take her by the shoulders and shake her hard. No response.

Rachel, Monica's little sister, pushes the door open just wide enough to fit her small, dark-eyed face through the threshold.

"What are you guys doing?"

"Nothing."

"What was that noise, then?" She slips through the door and kneels at the side of the bed next to me—mimicking my posture.

"We fell off the bed," Monica murmurs softly from her pillow, and I breathe again. "We were playing a game."

"What's wrong with her?"

"Nothing. She's sleeping. It's part of the game." Monica's eyes open now, heavy lidded.

"Did you faint her?" Rachel asks me.

"Yeah," Monica answers for me.

"Will you faint me, too?"

"Get out, Rachel."

"Yeah, Rachel. Get out," Monica says as if awakening from a spell.

"You guys suck," Rachel says, but leaves without threat. After the door shuts, Monica reaches out for my hand and I give it to her.

"There were all these flashes . . . like flashes from my life," she tells me, slurring a bit.

"What did you see?"

"Just little scenes. But really fast, like flipping channels. Not even long enough to do anything but feel them—"

"Feel what? The scenes?"

"Yeah, I *felt* the scenes—like everything was happening over again . . ."

"And?"

"And then I heard you talking and I went toward your voice and woke up."

"No, I mean, what kinds of feelings in the scenes?"

"Nothing, really. You know. Nothing important ever happens to me. Sad. Bored. Maybe a little angry . . ."

"See, that sounds like it sucks. I shouldn't have fainted you so long."

"No, it's good. I mean, the dream was kind of scary, but when I was coming out of it and could feel my body again it was way better than the first time—like all tingly and floating and really, really good everywhere— goose bumps everywhere. Do you think that's what heroin feels like?"

She isn't looking at me. She is looking deep into the ceiling. "Your dad's done heroin, right? Did he tell you what it feels like?"

"He didn't really say," I lie, "just that he puked the first time he shot up and knew he didn't want to do it again."

"I think I'd like to try it."

"That's stupid. It's really addictive. I mean, even *my dad* said he wouldn't do it again. You can get hooked, like, the first time you try it."

"Yeah."

"And then what if it turns out it feels nothing like fainting and you get addicted." My rhetoric is slipping. I look out into the blank night, the swath of concrete and the little stray patch of grass along the cyclone fence that is close enough to spit on—something twisting through the weeds. Do I remember it this way because of what happens later? How she learns to pull herself under without me—the people, like shadows, she goes under with—the rooms she needs to go deeper in to forget—the way I'll lose her—the way everyone will lose her—the way she'll emerge someone else.

"Yeah," she says dreamily, "but if it *does* feel like fainting—like floating—not really alive, but not really dead—" She turns to me to place her hand on my cheek.

"Will you do it again?"

Still Life with Summer Wasps

Our perspective dead-ends at a tall concrete wall built to keep out the sound of the semi trucks, their loads of timber and steel, charging down Going Street toward the shipping yards where some of our fathers work to box themselves away. We can hear the rush hour, but can't see it. Just before the wall, the access ramp spirals up to the overpass, a curve of metal rails to keep a body from going over, and at the center of the spiral is a pile of black garbage bags where something is rotting—sweet rot like a sickening vine, growing strong and wild—and for days we dare each other to walk past, holding our breath, not knowing what the stink means. Finally, the weight of her body splits the bags open—a corpse exposed to the rain.

We don't see her, but we hear about her from the cops combing the scene who tape off the site, look at us sideways, ask if we know anything about her *dead body*, and later that night on the evening news, just a clip of the newscaster's voice before my vigilant mother ushers me into the other room, saying, "You've seen enough for today"—the absence of the corpse's face worrying a hole in my mind.

No one tells me about being a woman, but I begin to see how it's done—the sad shape of my mother's mouth, the teachers with their frazzled hair, nervous hands, the women who stand on our corner to hitch a ride, their eyes like abandoned buildings, zombies. I begin to bleed, and walking to and from the bus stop I think of the boys at school growing stronger, trying to press me against lockers, wrap their fingers in my hair, slip their hands beneath my desk, and how it is harder to push them away. My guess at that dead girl's face drifted like stratus all through my overcast summer—the wan, moon-color of her skin, her dark, wind-knotted hair, wasps skimming her open eyes—no spirit loosed like a veil, no heaven opening to call her home, just the sound of the traffic thrumming down the interstate—*going . . . going . . . gone.*

The
Riots

The frame is what matters most, because outside of the frame we see nothing. The scene is blurred. It's night. The officers flash in and out, up and down, and Rodney King stays parallel with the pavement. Outside of the frame are the citizens of Los Angeles, staring out of their living room windows into the cool spring night, or letting the blue shift of the television screen strain their sleeping faces, their remote controls thumping to the floor, or they are waking from a terrible dream—their throats tense and dry—or who knows? Who knows what they are doing? Outside of the frame is a grown man, driving drunk and too fast on the freeway. Outside of the frame a married team of officers, Tim and Melanie Singer, turn on their siren to indicate that he should pull over, but instead of pulling over, he speeds up. This is suspicious. This is illegal. They speed up and he speeds up until their vehicles begin to rattle with the ache of speed—until they're in a *high-speed chase* over the Los Angeles freeway. Outside of the scene, the drunk man swerves toward an exit ramp, exits into a residential neighborhood, shows no signs of slowing. Outside of the frame, King's blood alcohol level is twice the legal limit. Someone turns over in her sleep, roused only slightly by the chase. Several dogs begin barking. Outside of the frame the Singers drive dangerously close to the vehicle, their siren screaming three other patrol cars and a helicopter behind them until they trap the vehicle and its crazed driver.

King's car is cornered, and when he emerges from the vehicle, he laughs pats the ground, waves to the police helicopter, grabs his own ass. Melanie draws her gun and orders King to lie on the ground, which he does, but the sergeant has arrived and orders her to holster her weapon. Outside of the frame, the sergeant orders a "swarm"—a technique in which multiple officers subdue a suspect by grabbing him with empty hands. King rises tossing two officers off of his back, strikes another in his chest, is manic and strong—too strong. Outside of the frame, the officers Taser the suspect—once, twice—he calls out as his body convulses. In the frame (the blurred frame of a handheld camcorder) the officers swarm around King sting with their batons.

＊

Just after the L.A. Riots were through, the principal of our school charged each homeroom class to attend a special meeting in the library, where we were encouraged to talk about our feelings. We were what the newscasters might call "at-risk youth." None of us had much to say. We'd all been laughing about it already—playing "slow motion riot" in the field on breaks, or saying, when any disagreement arose, "Can't we all just get along?" We threw cold tater tots at each other's heads in the lunchroom, calling them cinder blocks. We shot each other with our invisible automatic rifles—kicked in mimed store windows to steal the imaginary loot. The riots had been over only a week and already we'd seen the images so many times that they'd sunk into psychological obscurity—some back room of the mind. The teachers were disgusted with our response to the crisis, threatened us with detention, suspension, expulsion, but we just kept laughing, pretending to punch each other's faces.

"It's messed up," Alfonzo had finally spoken up. He usually played the clown, but this time there wasn't any joke in his voice. His brown cheek were a little lighter in the center, like a worn doorknob, and he puffed them out a little. We all nodded in agreement. David Aldez said he had cousins down there, and Elijah claimed he knew one of the rioters, who'd gotten away with a thousand dollars. He was clearly impressed.

After too long a silence, the teacher said that if we didn't feel like talking, then we'd watch the video. I was tired that day and kept my eyes closed for most of it, listening to the voices of the reporters with their slightly excited drone, and the windy staccato of the helicopters from which they viewed the footage. Occasionally, I could hear a gunshot or two beneath the helicopters, but mostly the riot was silent. Even in the clips of rioters shattering storefront windows with garbage cans, and the famous beatings where from hundreds of feet up, anyone could discern the violent hysteria of the crowds, *see* the broken limbs, the gunshot wounds, the faces smashed with cinderblocks, no one could hear it happen. It was always the same, even rhythm of the helicopter and the eager voices of the reporters swooping down to view the wreckage. *Vultures.*

I opened my eyes when I heard the first few chords of U2's "One"—a song I'd recently decided I liked—and watched some ground footage of a crowd in smoke and red dusk beating a man in slow motion—fire blazing at the edges of the frame. This was interrupted by the infamous footage of King's beating, also in slow motion, blurred and almost completely obscured by darkness—the horizontal blaze from the police car headlights illuminating the officers as they lowered their batons, stepped on King's prone body while Bono's famous voice ached over the scene, "You gave me nothing now it's all I've got."

"This is bullshit," Alfonzo's voice said softly behind me. "They're trying to make us cry." He sounded like he might cry when he said it. The video ended with the lumpy, dismayed face of Rodney King and the half-exhausted phrase we'd all been repeating. Then the video ended and we all stood, let the teacher shuffle us out of the dim library, back to our classroom, where we tried our best not to learn anything more that day.

Adam and I hadn't been close, so when he showed up on my porch a few days after he'd set our teacher's hair on fire, I was surprised to see him. It was raining and he wore a black hoodie (soaked through) that hid the top half of his face. When I walked out the front door, he sunk back a little, leaned on the porch railing. Behind his head, the tips of camellia leaves curled away into the dark.

"Hey, what's up," he said without looking at me. "It's cool that I'm here, right—not too late?" He looked hard at a corner of the porch where a small, dusty web clung—his hands sunk deep in his pockets. It was his usual posture. I wondered if he'd always stood that way, if he stood like that at his older brother's funeral, his mother leaning on his shoulder, already waning, already beginning to forget he was there.

He'd walked me home from school a few weeks before, but hadn't said much to me since. We didn't run in the same crowd, and earlier in the week I'd watched him escorted off the middle school grounds by police—cuffed and shoved into the back cab. He was looking at the pavement the whole time, his long, black hair running down his back.

"I thought I'd never see you again," I said.

"Why?"

"Why? *They took you away.* I was watching from a window."

"I'm a minor. It's not like I was going to Alcatraz." He had a way of making everything sound inconsequential.

"Well, what happens now?"

He smirked, "I figured we'd talk on your porch till your mom called you in."

"You know what I mean: what's going to happen *with you*?"

"Got expelled . . . and a court date."

"Like for jail?"

"Juvie? Don't know. I'll find out in court, I guess." He spit into the bushes, a habit.

"What's up with the hoodie? I can't see your face."

"That scare you—the big, bad Injun with his hoodie?"

"No."

"Not scared of me, huh?"

"Do you think I'd be out here if I was?"

"Maybe. People do weird shit when they're scared." He looked over the bushes into the dark rain.

"Like set people's hair on fire?" It took him off guard. He shifted to standing and looked straight at me.

"I don't get scared." He wasn't convincing.

"Mad? Annoyed?"

"No."

"Then what? You just went all pyro for no reason?" He spit into the bushes again.

"Dunno."

"You don't know?"

"No."

"You don't know or won't tell me?"

"Kinda both. You ask a lot of fucking questions."

I looked at my shoes, leaned against the shut door to take an unthreatening posture. Silence.

"Listen, you're the one who showed up here. I figured maybe you wanted to say something. There's no reason to get rude." I crossed my arms, the way my mother sometimes did, to show I was serious.

He took a breath and leaned against the railing again, slumping a little further into himself. Then he leaned back, looked up at the ceiling and wiggled his head so that his hood fell back. He looked at me with a small, tentative smile.

"Better?" he said. He had a soft face—brown and sweet, his mouth a little fuller than a boy's should be. But he had a way of keeping his expressions still. It made him hard to read.

"Was that an apology?"

He rolled his eyes, "What do I got to apologize about?"

"Probably a lot of things," I said. He laughed.

"You think you're pretty smart, don't you?"

"I don't think anything."

"Yeah you do. You probably think all the time. You probably calculate shit in your sleep."

"I'm bad at math."

"Yeah?" He sounded hopeful, "What's two times two?"

"Fuck you."

"That rhymed."

"I'm good at English." Three days ago we had been in the same English class.

He smiled wide, looked directly at me for a moment, then back at his shoes.

"I know," he said after a while, then got up from the rail and walked past me, "I gotta go now."

"Really? Why?"

"It's getting late. I got a mom, too." I pictured a woman with dark hair and a round face (like his) peeling carrots and weeping in a dim kitchen. He was already in the dark when he said, "See ya."

"Wait." I walked into the rain toward his shadowy form. "Are you coming back?"

"Maybe."

"When?"

"I don't know."

"Well . . . you don't have to, but if you want to talk about it, you can talk about it with me."

"I know," he said, "but I don't know."

"Don't know what?"

"Why I did it."

"You really don't know?"

"You always got a reason for the things you do?"

I shrugged, "Guess not." That was good enough for him. He pulled his hood over his head (his face), then darted into the dark.

✴

At thirteen, my body felt contaminated. I itched with it. Worse, other people began to notice. I'd stand at the bus stop in the rain with my jeans soaked through, my backpack gaining weight, and grown men in white family sedans—the men who pulled over for the women at the corner—began to pull over for me. They'd roll down their windows and lean out, ask how much money to get me into their cars—rain always falling on their coiffed hair, their slightly yellowed smiles, their wedding rings. *You don't want to stand all day in the rain, do you?* Where did those men come from? They had business suits and a way of speaking, so I knew they weren't from the neighborhood. There were other men who stopped, who seemed closer to home—the men in beat-up vans with missing teeth. They'd say *Get in and fuck me*—their hands already down their pants.

"Go fuck *yourself*," I'd learned to say, but I believed there must be something wrong with me. Why else would they look at me and think what they did? And the boys at school were only worse—how they trapped me in crowds in corners just to see what I would do if they touched me. And Richard had begun to sit next to me in every class we had together. Richard with his slick-backed hair and sharp, Polish nose, who liked to lean in with his hand on my thigh and whisper in my ear, *I'm going to rape you. I'm going to knock you out, put a bag over your ugly face, and fuck you in my bathtub.* The bathtub, he explained, was so I didn't bleed on his sheets—he surmised that I was still a virgin.

I was a good girl—quiet and submissive. I did what the teachers told me to do, what my father and mother told me to do, and even cursing at those men at the bus stop stuck inside me like ice. Everyone seemed to be saying, *Keep your mouth shut, take it, and it will be over soon.* Only once did I try to move to another seat, and when I couldn't explain why I was moving (how could I repeat what he'd said?) I was escorted by the crook of my arm back to my seat and given detention. *You can't protest your fate*. Each day, I came home from school crying, and my mother worried over me, asking what was wrong, but I could never tell her the whole truth (how could I repeat what he said?), and in the end I swallowed it down like metal. Outside of the frame, at night, I dreamed of knives. Otherwise, I couldn't sleep and stayed up listening to my mother lose every fight.

   ✦

Downstairs, my father is screaming drunk. He's been screaming all night. It's dead-dark and my little sisters, who ran to my bed when the fighting began, have fallen asleep from exhaustion. My mother's voice is calmer— rises through the floorboards as murmur, as prayer. The prayers are met with pounding, shouting, some wooden thing smashed. It started when my mother put herself between my father and brother. Where my brother was now, I couldn't say—in his room, perhaps. I don't hear his voice. I'm listening for signs of peace, but for a long time nothing lets up. I hear my father say *whore*. He means my mother, and the coals in my throat ignite. My mother is modesty embodied—is Our Lady of Guadalupe—is the one who stays up crying at the window, waiting for him to come home. He says, "You fucking bitch," and I hear hard things (books?) hitting the walls. My mother yells, "Stop, please stop." My father says, "Why don't you just go back to your rich boy, you pregnant whore." My mother isn't pregnant and hasn't been for years. He means my mother fifteen years ago—pregnant with another man's baby the day they met—the woman he married to save. He wanted to be a hero. "Go see if he still wants you and your retarded son, you ungrateful bitch." Then my mother screams, twice. I get up from the bed, careful not to wake my sisters—let them fold into the empty space I leave—tiptoe out of the door, down the hall, and down the stairway.

    When I turn the corner into the hall, I face my father's back, so it is my mother's face I see first and she's surprised—her eyes, red and swollen, say *Leave right now before he sees you*. But already he's turning around.

She shakes her head *no*, reaches out her hands, but already he's backing down the hallway—already his body is tense with rage, made larger by the way he charges forward while I stumble back in the bathroom, the dry bathtub—already he's slammed and locked the door, his gigantic hands on my throat—already he is multiplied by the way he throttles me (the room buzzing, going in and out of view), saying, "We're splitting up, so choose between us. You better choose right." I try to scream but he tightens his grip on my throat. "Answer me right now: which one of us do you choose?" I can't answer. My knees fold beneath me and I feel my body slide down into the cold tub. Just before the room goes dim, he releases my throat. He stands over me a minute while I cough and sob as quietly as I can (my hands over my mouth), then unbolts the door and walks through it. *You can't protest your fate.*

Because this was the first day of the riots and he was home, shut in, watching the mob on his television as he listened to them outside his door, and because the scene was happening a half mile away. Because, perhaps, he was tired of being accused. Because he was not a *beast*, not a *lawless criminal*, not the marked, marred black man that flashed across his screen day in, day out. Because he couldn't just sit there watching, was sick to watch. Because his bones said *get up* and the sun was setting and he wouldn't be swept away in fear or anger. Because he couldn't sit or stand above it and feel his place in the world. Because he was not a trembling creature. Because he had a clear view of justice. Because he knew on which street the crowd had stopped the white truck driver, dragged him from his vehicle, beat him unconscious with concrete fragments and cinderblocks while news helicopters hovered above, recording every blow, as he lay unconscious in the street. Because he knew the police wouldn't come, having been ordered to withdraw for their own safety. Because he'd seen enough, Bobby Green Jr. went out through the crowd to the scene where he met three others of the same mind. Because they fought off the crowd, returned the white stranger to his truck, got into the truck cab and drove him to the hospital, that man is still alive.

For months, the pundits and editors wrote on the root causes of the riots: poverty, segregation, lack of education, drug addiction, deteriorating family structure, widespread perceptions of police abuse, prejudiced juries, Los Angeles's growing ethnic diversity, immigration, unequal commerce, and a general sense of unavoidable failure in the eyes of the white hegemony. "How is it possible," Midge Decter wrote in *Commentary*, "to go on declaring that what will save the young men of South-Central L.A., and the young girls they impregnate, and the illegitimate babies they sire, is jobs? How is it possible to look at these boys of the underclass . . . and imagine that they either want or could hold on to jobs?" Outside of the frame, everyone forms a theory. The frame is never included in the theory, and no one includes themselves.

What I had to say couldn't be said. What I wanted to say got caught in my throat, or otherwise dissipated from my tongue—became the white breath of cold mornings. That late April the weather was moody and the days were tenuous. We were all feared storms, or riots, and scurried around like beetles. The teachers were watchful in the classrooms. The principal patrolled the halls. The adults were afraid of us and we felt it, and it made us afraid of ourselves—we were callous, lawless, criminals in waiting. The city had thrown us all into one place to make sure we didn't bother the good citizens.

We would never be the good citizens. We were what they called "at risk youth," and only the toughest took up our cause. I say *our* when I mean to say *they*. Because I looked white and bookish—kept my voice to myself—everyone believed I belonged elsewhere. Even the small group of friends I prized assumed that I'd leave them someday. I also assumed I'd leave the throng, and felt guilty for my future escape. Why didn't they believe they'd leave? Why didn't they want to come with me? They saw themselves tied to a fate I would refuse, and while refusing, I would lose them. But the guilt went deeper than that. It settled in a glaze on my skin, and stung and stung until I felt half-crazed with guilt—wanted to apologize to every dark face that passed mine. Instead, I crept inside myself and didn't let on, and didn't fight back. The girls in the bathroom who'd hold me down, place their bare, sweaty feet on my face. The boys who'd punch me in the stomach for walking down the halls. *I deserve it. I deserve it. Just take it and it will be over soon.* It was important to me not to fight back. Still, I watched the riots with trembling fascination, and for months after, when the reporters spoke of the *underlying causes*, I couldn't help but think that they meant me.

Out in the field, a black boy and white boy have pummeled each other and are crying. They are rocks dropped into still water and the peripheral crowd ripples out, angry, turns toward the brick wall I'm standing against. The sky is a spring crucible—something transforming there—and all the dark bodies in their dark coats spread wide over the field then snap back together, become a singular gesture of fists. I have been running laps and stopped here, am still trying to catch my breath and when I see what's coming toward me I lose it again. *Maybe that's good*, I think, *maybe if I don't breathe, if I can't speak, if they don't notice me standing here, if I look at the ground.* But when the crowd gets close one boy juts out, thrusts his face in mine, says, "What are you looking at, bitch?" He says *bitch*, hard like hammer on a table, like a life sentence, like he meant it. My eyes flicker up (I think maybe if he sees I mean no harm he'll let me be) and that's enough to enrage him, he presses my shoulder to the brick, his nose to my nose, screams so loud his face trembles (I can feel the small spray of his spit, the breath from his mouth pushing into my mouth), and slams his fist against the brick near my ear again and again throughout the long scream. When he's through with me he tries to step back but the whole crowd has pressed in around us like water and a voice reaches up to ask, "What did she do?"

The boy yells, turning to the crowd, "She called me *nigger*! She looked right at me and called me nigger!" What's worse is he's beautiful. What's worse is his skin is perfect, his cheekbones shine in his lean face. What's worse is I'd been half in love with this boy all year, carrying his name around in my mouth, *wanted* him to be this close to me—prayed for it. This thought glints in, then glints out.

"No, I didn't—" I say, but it's lost in the voice of the crowd, which has risen all around itself, sudden and shimmering—a tsunami. "I didn't—I would never—" but now the crowd needs to touch me, hurt me a little—the crowd's hands on my body, rolling me over the wall against the steel door, slipping down the neck of my sweater, over my hips and thighs, punching my side (that deep ache in the ribs), a hard slap to the side of my head. My ear rings. I press back into the door (the cold bar against my back) and fall so easily through, but there's a corner with an overhang of stairway, and I get caught there in the slant-space, and the crowd is mercurial, spills in with me—my back against the *V* of the corner. I hold my arms out in front of me and the crowd forms a wall of bodies just at the tips of my fingers. The boy I think I love is no longer in sight. *Please don't let him hate me.* The bustle slows to a pause when the bell rings—everyone's eyes glancing slightly up during the long, high-pitched ache.

I hear Dominique's voice a few layers back ask, "Danielle? Is that you?"

"Yes," I say as flatly as I can. She moves her arms forward and through the crowd as if swimming to the front—her brown, oval face, her arched eyebrows.

"What did you do?" She's confused. Someone from the front row standing next to her says, "He says she called him nigger." Her face switches from confusion to suspicion, but not certainty. She doesn't know me well. But now the arms of the crowd are mostly quiet, hang loosely, and the bodies have halted, and the voices are quiet. Some faces look as if they just woke up. They are ready to pay attention, to entertain questions.

"You called him nigger?"

"No. No. I've never called anyone that in my life."

"Who is that up there?" Now it's Riga's voice from beyond the threshold of the doorway yelling in, "Who you all got up against the wall?"

"Some girl that called a boy nigger," someone replies.

"Oh, *shit*. I got to see this! You all got to move. Move now! Riga's coming through," she says, swimming to the front of the crowd. Riga is thick, short, and dark as midnight on a new moon. Everything about her is powerfully round—her arms, her eyes, her face, her voice—and there is the sense that when she walks an invisible second self clears the way before her. She looks straight at me like she always does.

"Danielle? How you get here, girl?" Someone in the crowd repeats again the single sentence, *She called him nigger*. "I *heard* that *thank you*. I don't need to hear it again. What I'm saying is this can't be right." Then she leans in closer and whispers in my ear, "It's not right, right?"

"Riga," I say her name like I always do. She smiles into my face, then turns around, raises her arms as if she's giving a great speech.

"You all got it wrong here. This white girl is cool." And for further proof she adds, "She can sing," then brushes the air with her fingertips to shoo the crowd away. "Nothing to see here, folks. Everyone go back to class." But someone interrupts, confused: "You friends with this white girl?"

"What I'm saying is she's all right. She's not *all* white and besides she can sing."

"That white girl can sing?" someone else asks.

"Yes. This white girl can sing like a black girl, so you got to know she's no bigot. Go ahead, Danielle," she says turning toward me, "Show 'em you can sing."

My throat is summer pavement—my tongue slightly numb, and I am still trembling. I try to protest.

"Now, come on, girl, you got a good voice and everything's alright now and everyone here want to hear a song."

Sing something! Sing something! Sing something!

"You probably wouldn't like any of the songs I sing," I say, but now the people at the back of the crowd outside hear what's happening and push into the corridor (spilling down the hall) to hear the announced performance. I stay where I am, shaking my head *no*.

Sing something! Sing something!

"Don't make me look like a liar. Come on, now, Danielle, you got to sing them something."

I nod my head, breathe in, breathe out. The people in front turn away to shush the people in back, and when the shush gets to the end of the crowd everyone turns forward, leans in a little. I imagine the gray sky produces a gold pearl of light. The squall through the forest at the center of my body suddenly ceases whipping through the boughs. I realize I have no choice. I close my eyes and sing.

Wildflowers line the edge of the bluff that marks the border between our neighborhood and the industrial valley. In some spots, the bluff is only a hill with a broad, steep face—in others, it's a swift drop down. We used to go there in there in the evening—after school, before curfew—to watch the lights turn on in the valley, and across the valley, up into the steep rise on the distant other side, where mansions hung like lit fruit in the West Hills.

"Look at those rich motherfuckers," Adam said, holding up his broad, flat hands to frame the view. Though his back is to me, I imagine his black eyes squinted—almost closed. Morgan had already picked up a rock and tossed it up in the air, caught it, tossed it again—eyebrows knit together— his narrow shoulders hunched forward like a bulldog. I was sure he'd seen this posture somewhere before, and was trying it on. His father, probably—when he leaned in to hit him. We all knew that was why Morgan liked fighting. Even then, at twelve or thirteen, I could see him willing himself into a kind of violence.

"Fuck them." Morgan said it quietly. Bobby, who only shifted into his best fighting pose when prompted by Adam or Morgan, didn't catch on yet. He was staring into the now yellow and silver afterglow of sunset, his brown skin shining a little golden—arms folded across his chest. I knew he had a little crush, and stood closest to me on the left. On my right, Morgan tossed his stone, and further to my right, on the very edge of the cliff, Adam's long frame leaned forward—his stiff black hair hanging to the middle of his back. Morgan threw his rock. Adam swung around with his fists already balled.

"What the fuck, Morgan?! You almost hit me, you bitch!" Morgan broke his tough-guy pose to laugh—a high-pitched giggle—and ran behind me.

"Oh, you're going to hide behind a girl?! You *are* a bitch, aren't you, you little bitch!"

"Woo-hoo! Adam's mad . . . *mad*! And now Danielle's mad, too!" Morgan threw punches randomly out from my sides, as if his arms were part of my body, "Look, she has four arms, and two of them are mad!" The anger melted from Adam's face.

"You *fool*," he said, smiling a little. "You fuckin' *clown*."

"It's fucked up that you ran behind a girl," Bobby offered. He was always a little late.

"Oh, and what the fuck did you do? Nothing. And what would you do if I threw a rock and it *did* hit your head? Nothing. You probably wouldn't even feel it."

"Shut up." That was the best Bobby could come up with. His jaw jutted out a little when he was hurt. He was always getting the short of it from the other two. Almost anything he said was up for possible humiliation, except his dad (a disabled Vietnam Vet) and his mom (a Vietnamese immigrant)—the boys let that be.

"What are we doing?" I said, finally, to Adam, who was leaning down into the wildflowers now, picking up rocks.

"Getting ammunition."

"For what?"

"Fucking up the rich people."

"I think we should go home."

"Not *for real*, you fuckin' sissy. You Goody Two-Shoes." He said *Good Two-Shoes* while prancing, as if he were riding a delicate horse—"we're just gonna put a little Indian voodoo on their asses."

"You don't know any voodoo."

"Cherokee know strong voodoo. Make rich white man pee from ass."

"And I don't think it's called *voodoo* when Cherokees do it."

"Oh, yeah? What's it fuckin' called then, smarty pants—you don't even know what we're doing yet."

"Don't you need some sort of a doll?" Bobby said behind me.

"It's not that kind of voodoo," Morgan said toward the earth, squatting in a thicket of bright perennials.

"You want a doll?! You want a little dolly?" Adam taunted.

"*You* want a doll," Bobby tried.

"Nice comeback. Good work, Bobby. *Yur real smart, arencha kid*?" Adam liked to ask this in his John Wayne accent.

"Fuck you."

"I'll bet you want to. I knew you were gay."

"So *what are we doing*, then?" I said, annoyed.

"*Now just hold yur horses there, lil' lady*. Slow the fuck down. Don't get all hormonal on me. We're going to need your concentration."

"For what?"

"Have I been talking to myself over here? What did I just say?"

"Voodoo."

"Right. Jesus. This cliff got an echo to it?"

"I mean, what are we doing with the rocks?"

"We're going to throw them across the bluff and break every one of those fuckers' windows."

"That's not voodoo. It's vandalism."

"*Vandalism.* What are you, a cop?"

"I'm just saying . . ."

"Don't get your fuckin' period on me. It's not for real. We're pretend ing. We're *using our imaginations*, like Mr. Rogers wants us to. You good with that?"

I nodded. By now, Bobby and Morgan had formed a small pile of rocks near the guard rail. We stood around it.

"Now what?" I said. He picked up a rock from the pile, turned his body so that he half-faced us and half-faced the cliff.

"You gotta let the rock settle in your palm, all loose. Then squint your eyes, so the houses look small instead of far—like you could crush them between your fingers. Then—" he threw the stone as hard as he could, letting out a little grunt when he did it, and his momentum pulled him a few steps forward to the edge of the bluff. He flapped his arms to keep steady— keep from going too far. Once he had his balance he turned around—the whole industrial valley swooning below him—and said, "like that."

"This is stupid," I said, but didn't turn away. Adam shrugged, swooped down to pick up another rock.

It was getting dark and one by one the mansion windows were lighting up, impossibly large and bright. I stood there on the edge of the bluff, imagining the people inside eating chocolate, playing cellos, planning their trips to Paris. Some sharp thing heated up inside me. My bet was none of them had fathers like mine. All their men were so clean, certain—it was even possible I'd met some of them—that some of those grown men from the bus stop who wanted to pay to hurt me could have just driven over the bridge with their fat wallets. With their fat eyes and their stupid smiles. With their stupid fucking smiles and the way they talked like they were doing me a favor—*you don't want to just stand here in the rain, do you?*—as if the choice they offered was *better* than standing there in the rain—as if they were saving me from my sad position. As if they were heroes. That itch I'd been carrying around with me—that contamination—started to burn in my skin, sizzle the top of my head. And I liked it. I liked standing there getting angry, staring at the people we couldn't see whose lives seemed easy and clean and full of frivolous choices. My heart pounded. Adam placed a handful of rocks in my hand.

"We'll fuck them up," he said, as if reading my mind, "We'll give them a fucking riot. Throw as hard as you can. Aim for their teeth."

I threw one stone as hard as I thought I could.

"Don't be a girl. You can hit them harder."

I threw one harder.

"Harder!"

Then we all started throwing the stones, letting out great yelps and screams, sometimes turning to the confused faces of the people driving past at the bend in the road. They looked worried, as if they might stop to say something, but they always turned at the bend in the road, toward their lives outside of the frame, and we kept throwing and throwing. It didn't mean anything, and we didn't have a reason. We didn't know. We didn't know why. But the stones were as light and as heavy as birds, and it was fine to throw them—to squint our eyes and imagine them flying across the valley through the dark to the close, untouchable mansions—striking every one of those windows out.

Cadena

Over the phone my grandfather's words are thick and slow like smoke from a damp fire—it is only when he breaks into Spanish that the words take on heat:

"Which one is this?"

"This is Danielle."

"Ahh. Daniela. Are you good for your mother?"

"Yes, Abuelo."

"She says you are muy inteligente. Are you a smart one?"

"Um. Well, sometimes."

His deep laugh rolls.

"*Sí*, yes. Sometimes me, too. Sometimes not. Now, maybe not. I am growing too old to be smart."

"You're smart!"

"No. Gloria all the time tells me I am estupido, and she knows everything todo el mundo, and besides I did not go to . . . ah, to La Universidad, ah, for the college."

"To college?"

"Sí. To college. Are you going to college?"

"I'm not old enough yet."

"Ah si, yes. But, when you are older?"

"Yes."

"Good. Bueno. Escuela es muy importante, so you do not grow to be an old man who did not go to college."

"I can't turn into an old man; I'm a girl."

He laughs again. "I know that! I am smarter at least to know *that*!"

"See, you're smart!"

"Oh, well . . . when will you come to see me?

"I don't know. When my dad takes me?"

"Where is your dad?"

"Right here. Do you wanna talk to him?"

"No. No. Ask him when he will be a good son-in-law, and bring my beautiful granddaughters to Los Angeles to see me."

"Hey, Dad, Grandpa wants to know when you'll take us to see him."

"When I have the money."

"He says when he has the money."

"Ask him when he will have the money."

"Grandpa wants to know when you'll have the money."

"I don't know."

"He doesn't know."

"Tell him he should bring mi familia to Los Angeles. We will drink tequila and speak Español."

"Grandpa says if you come to L.A. you can drink tequila and speak Spanish with him . . . Can you speak Spanish, Dad?

"No."

"He says he can't speak Spanish."

"Ah, but eh-Spanish is easier than Ingles. He can speak eh-Spanish! If he drinks enough tequila he can speak eh-Spanish. I will give him a stupid sombrero on his head. He can walk around en mi casa with his big stupid hat, drinking tequila and speaking eh-Spanish. Tell him if he can marry mija Cecilia, *my only daughter*, he can do at least that."

Childhood

Dad keeps his gun in his sock drawer. Instead of cowboy boots I wear the galoshes my cousin outgrew and pretend they are cowboy boots. Great-grandmother Mars is about to die but none of us know it. It is overcast outside but we want to swim anyway. Bijam has dark hair and big dark eyes and says his name is French like mine and also we are the same height so that is good. At Ryderwood Lake, my father fishes from a dock while my brother and I look for salamanders. I like to think the hazelnut orchard is magic and each time I am disappointed. I shove my face into the barrel of fresh dill at the farmers' market. The best we can hope for is he'll get so drunk he'll fall asleep on the couch and we can tiptoe around until Mom comes home. Everyone is gathered at Thanksgiving and eats the usual things. I pluck the soft leaves and press them to my face, pretending they are something to take care of. When Dad walks through the door his eyes are red and we know to scatter. In the funeral parlor I think of how bright she seemed at dinner—talking more than usual—and how I thought that meant she wanted to live. Dad says, *I'm sorry, I'm so sorry*, but he's not. The creek is opaque, muddy, full of sawdust (a beaver downstream, our grandfather tells us), and I'm afraid of crawdads pinching my toes. Dad's in the bedroom with the door half-shut, snorting white powder from a mirror. We eat from the garden until we are sick to our stomachs. Bijam brings me little fistfuls of dandelions and bluebells that are half-crushed by the time he delivers them. My father asks me to sing, so I do, and after, he insists everyone give me money, which embarrasses me. We can't afford cowboy boots. I know better than even to ask. Hours and hours "playing quietly" in the back room with a Scrabble board and small record player and only two albums. If Dad wants to (and sometimes he wants to) he throws a lamp or end table against the wall just to smash it. It's the greenness of the scent—the unabashed sunniness of it—that I love. My father tells us if we rub the salamander's belly it will fall asleep in our hands but I think it's something else. Zinnias in the u-pick field. Above the casket, *a hawk*. My cousin said it was a sign her spirit was at peace, but I knew it was a turkey vulture. Dad yelling from his bedroom window, waiving around his gun. Can't untangle my ankles from the cucumber vines. They sold that property—it exists elsewhere now. I was always just waiting for someone to say I could eat the pumpkin pie. A green-bean tepee in the backyard where my sister and I take turns being queen. The evening sprinklers start up like gossip over the dry lawns. My mother is angry at me and my mother is never angry at me; she kicks my pew and tells me, "Shut up right now," but I can't stop laughing. My father sees I'm bored and sends me out to the field and I return with flowers but he says it's not enough to please a girl like me—I need more, go get more. I tell my brother to shut up but he won't listen until Dad drags him screaming into his room. Where is the old woman who always keeps one yellow eye on her nectarine tree? Dad comes home with a new Buick and fur coats for all us girls. Our old dog, Gypsy, is dying and dying—bare patches of skin in her long red hair—but still stands up and wags when she sees me. My sister and I play John the Baptist, drenching each other in the muddy tide. Dill and also lilac from our front yard and my mother's cedar hope chest. I dream, again, of finding the corpses of the people my father has killed. Everything is brown—wood-paneled walls and outside a hazelnut orchard. Bored out of my mind. The grasses sway. I'm not sure I know what *birthstones* are supposed to do but I think it must be something pretty special. Bijam is a new boy at school and I'm supposed to meet him in the office and escort him to our class. He aims for my chest and I place my hand there. My brother searches too close to the edge and falls in, his eyes all panic, his hands like claws. We hold invisible scepters. Before the ceremony a bad singer sings over the intercom and my cousin and I smash our hands against our faces to keep from laughing but everyone glares our way. My fever is so high my body trembles. Kari Joy has chicken pox too, so we get to stay home together and play in the backyard. Church people bring us baskets of food for Thanksgiving and my sisters and I dance around the netted clementines. Mom's screaming downstairs and I'm scared he's hurting her, so I run down to save her but I don't save her. We know to hold them carefully and not for long as so not to injure them. I'm very glad I wore my purple corduroy jumper and crimped my hair this morning. My best friend yells "Kiss her, kiss her," and Bijam's eyes get big and his face turns red. Dad teaches me to harvest the marijuana—*money trees*, he calls them. I fall in after my brother and swallow too much of the lake or the lake swallows too much of me, either way I am terrified. Wish-seeds float in the air all summer and we think if we catch them. My cousin and I make up a dance to Pat Benatar's "Love is a Battlefield" and plan to perform it for the whole neighborhood but don't. That was a stupid idea; no one can stop him. On long drives, Mom and Dad hold hands and sing along to the love songs on the radio—they are good at making up. Pomegranates are my favorite but they're only a winter fruit, so I settle for nectarines or (if I've been good) artichokes. Dad backs me through the hallway into the dry bathtub, where he crushes my throat in his large hands. Bijam presses his mouth to my mouth for two seconds. The tall pines sway and tremble in the rain, the clouds like curtains over what comes next. I dream of one day owning garnets, which according to my mother is my birthstone. One of the albums plays "Stand by Your Man" and my cousin and I twirl over the brown carpet, imaginary men in our arms. He grips my throat until I slide into the tub, everything turning black. I fall off of the stairway and miss the burning wood stove, land face-first on the brick floor beside it. When I open my eyes he's running across the blacktop to the other side of the playground and it's not until he reaches the other side that he turns around, sees that I have been watching him, waves hello (goodbye?).

Still Life with Doldrums

Nothing but layers of blue—the sky and water both as warm as the veins beneath a thin-skinned wrist. Sapphire. Turquoise. Aquamarine. The opalescent sky and the sleeping water. Not a single breath of wind ripples the surface. The ocean lies there like a mirror. I think of laundry washed and folded, empty cupboards, clear glass vases lined up on a sill—whatever came before us was erased. No wake. Not even the memory of a wake—the water a teal tombstone worn down by time, by silence. No names. We're dead center of the Atlantic and in all directions the clean-slate sky, the stoic water. I lean against the starboard rail and let my body fold forward a bit, try to stare through the surface, but all I see is myself reflected back at me, a little cooler, a little glossier. *This is death*, I think, imagining the slow thirst of sailors, their slack sails hanging like great sickly eyelids, lime-water fetid in barrels. And down in the belly of the ship, captives weak from hunger—the slow stir of their thin limbs in the darkness, the slick green darkness, their open wounds against iron, musk-rot, fever, the ammonia of urine. *No.* I lean back to solid footing on the whitewashed planks, breath in. There's no wind here, but I shiver. *And if they died, were they left in the hull among the live people, or thrown out to sea?* I think, and then, *Why don't*

I know this? Why don't I know my own country's history? Maybe I hadn't been paying attention until now. Maybe I didn't want to know. Bone in the water. The sky is blank. I squint at the slim horizon, looking for some hint of land, feel an itch on my palm, look to see what's etched there—tributaries. As a child, my work was swimming the muddy Columbia, through oil-swirls and grit—one eye on my slight sisters, one on the uneven shore. But like all work, I tired—swam away to the buoys, bright orange in the sun where the rush was harder to swim against, and sometimes I let myself drift downstream, closing my eyes against the glare. My father, always leathering his skin on shore, sometimes lifted his blue eyes toward the water to watch the wakes of boats and daughters. Even then, I was planning my escape.

Prodigal Daughter

"It's just that you never came back home," Jasmine says, looking up briefly at the window, then back to her hands on her knees.

It's that dreary time between Christmas and New Year's, and I'm due back to Virginia before the year is up. Throughout my visit to Portland, the sky is perpetually grey, latent with rainfall, or raining, and my sister is pale for lack of sunlight. She's sitting at the corner of her living room futon with her slender legs folded beneath her. Her delicate face is wan with dark eyebrows that pull together when she's sad.

Flames burning low in her fireplace reveal the charcoaled shapes of whatever it was she no longer wanted. Her voice is calm and her words are brave, but her eyebrows betray her: she's angry with me.

I stare into the fire a while, then up at the window. The sun is setting and each time I look out, the street is darker. Soon I won't be able to see anything outside, just the distance between our postures and faces reflected in the glass. She's in one corner and I'm in the other, and when she says, "Why don't you come home?" I think, *Why don't you leave?*

"It's just that I have a life somewhere else," I try.

"And why can't you make a life here?"

She feels abandoned, and I've begun to think of how long this dynamic has been seething beneath us. She was too young to remember everything that happened. The moments of our childhood come back to her like ghosts—vague shapes out of context, no beginning, no end. *Our house was a curse*—I want to tell her. *It never leaves me.* Some nights, walking alone through rainy city streets, scenes return to me in flashes so potent they strangle everything that comes after—cause a brief, partial amnesia. For an instant, the present moment is erased, but the past emerges, furious and breathing. *I'm always half-home.*

The sun is gone now, the streetlights have come on, and neither of us has turned on a lamp. She's waiting for an answer, but the answer is cruel— *I had the chance to leave, so I took it.* We sit in her living room, at the bottom of a deep, silent trench with what's left unsaid between us.

❦

I'm insomnia-dazed and vibrating in the back of the bus, wondering how far I have to go to really feel gone. The open windows let in the scents and sounds of southern India. Chennai is a montage of heat and sensory abundance. Seawater hangs heavy on the air, dotting the windowpanes and bright umbrellas with humidity, gleaming on the melons stacked in wooden carts and the coats of wild oxen as they lounge in the street. I could swear the sultry air turns the women's saris darker—a thousand shades of emerald, turquoise, lavender, vermillion, apricot—slicking the slim yellow taxis, sliding down the brown chests of rickshaw drivers, and even the police, with their faces of ammunition, their wrinkled tan uniforms and their thumbs tucked beneath the straps of guns, have a mix of coal dust and salt-water in their hair. Long garlands of jasmine, fuschia, and roses hang over barefoot sleepers shrouded in filthy blankets—turmeric, coriander, sweat, smoke, dung, burning oil, green plantains, and boxes of incense, women whose hips lean against doorways, their black braids oiled and thrown over their shoulders. Half-naked roving children chase the slow buses along storefronts. They scream and leap and pick each other up.

My bus halts at a corner. The children rush to the windows, curling their small, brown fingers over the sills. One child touches my arm, and when I look down, I see my sister, Jasmine. I shake my buzzing head. I look down again and there she is—the face of my sister, so long ago when she was a child, but somehow darker—Jasmine dipped in molasses. She grins up at me, her skinny chest flaring caramel in the sun, and places her flat palm in front of me. But before I can touch the coins and bills I know are consorting at the bottom of my bag, the bus lurches forward and she's quick to snap her hands back, squeal a laugh as she jumps away into the crowd of dark arms that enfold her completely like a river.

It's August, nearly dawn, and all night I haven't slept. The balm of cut grass and rhododendrons drifts through my open window and I listen to the cars on the interstate thrumming toward and away. My dreams have been full of foreboding and now I'm afraid to close my eyes. I throw back my covers and sit up, look at the clock—5:14 a.m. Still dark. *I need to get out of this house.*

To get out of my room I have to walk through Jasmine's room, and she's a light sleeper. I consider jumping out of my window but when I lean out of it, I swoon a little and change my mind. Instead, I dress in the dark and slip out of my door, down the short hall, and past Jasmine's bed to the top of the stairs and the beads that serve as her doorway. When I try to step through, the beads rattle and Jasmine sits straight up in her bed, asks me what I'm doing.

"Can't sleep. Going for a walk."

"I'm coming with you," she says to my surprise. "I can't sleep, either."

Before our father remodeled the second half of the attic into a separate space for me, Jasmine and I shared the territory—a border taped down the center of the room. Our beds were continents, our wooden floor, the sea. When we fought, which was often, we were assigned to stay silent in our beds until we could apologize, but that hardly seemed fair to me—silence was easy for Jasmine.

I begged and begged for my own room, and finally our parents gave in. Our father framed a new room in the attic, hammered up new walls, textured the ceiling like clouds, and laid down carpet. He picked out wallpaper of primary-colored hearts and fashioned a rainbow window between my sister's room and mine, so when her light was on, the rainbow glowed. Jasmine and I divided up our few belongings, and said goodbye with pleasure.

But that first night tucked away, it seemed, on either side of the world, I couldn't sleep. When we shared a room I could blame her for keeping me awake, but now the space seemed immense, filled my wide eyes until early in the morning, when Jasmine opened my door with her arms full of bedding. We made a nest of blankets on the floor and fell asleep, our fingers tangled.

There were many nights after that we'd slept that way, but we were older now, and space stretched out between us. We began to see our father in a larger context—had friends whose fathers didn't behave as he did—who didn't smash the furniture, or throttle a brother at the slightest provocation—but talking about what had happened, what was happening, made the constant threat of him more real, and I preferred to stay silent. I sank farther and farther into the faraway places of the books that I read, and she disappeared inside her drawings. We hardly spoke anymore.

She throws a large blue hoodie over her pajamas (loose over her skinny body) and grabs a pair of flip-flops. We step down the stairs together very slowly, avoiding the creaky spots and holding our shoes in our hands as we tiptoe through the living room where our youngest sister, Mileah, always sleeps on the couch. She stirs a little, murmuring something in her sleep, her dark hair falling across her face, but we make it to the front door. I unbolt and unlatch the door so that it barely makes a click, and when we reach the front porch without having been caught, we look at each other, amazed.

She smiles and whispers, "I can't believe no one woke up."

I whisper back, "Why are we whispering? We're outside." She laughs with her hand over her mouth.

"Where are we going?"

"I didn't think that far ahead."

"Then let's just walk."

We walk a mile down Concord Street through the neighborhood, falling into a comfortable rhythm of conversation and silence. Nothing of great importance is said. I make stupid jokes and she laughs. She points out things in the landscape I wouldn't have otherwise noticed. She's always had a keen eye for detail, and can draw anything she sees—never took lessons, just knew how. She could spend hours and hours on the floor curled over a sheet of paper, everyone walking and talking around her, her intense gaze fixed on the lines she created. Once she set her mind to something, it was impossible to distract her from it.

She plucks a bright yellow, star-shaped flower from someone's wilting flowerbed and holds it in front of her face like a mask, though it barely covers the width of her nose. We both smile—it's a joke only she and I share. Her middle name is Star, and as a kid I liked to point out things that shared her name:

"Look: it's you," I'd say, pointing to a star fruit, a starfish, the night sky.

She'd shake her head, say, "No, I'm here."

"But how can you be here, when you're there?"

It's a script we've reduced to gesture—a star anywhere means *Jasmine Star*.

Eventually, she lets her flower-hand drop to her side, and somewhere along the way, the blossom falls from her fingers. When we arrive at the elementary school, we wander onto the playground's blacktop. In the middle of the grounds there's a huge steel climbing dome the height of a house and we climb to the top of it, dangle our feet over the mounds of sawdust. We watch the sun rise there—up over the roofs of the dark brick buildings, through the shredded basketball nets, onto the pavement where the white paint of the boundary lines is illuminated.

"I can't believe we got out of there without getting caught," she says.

"Yeah—as it turns out, you just go."

Jasmine swims lazily in the pool, in and out of the shade, her slim form buoyant and lithe, her wavy, honey-colored hair drifting behind her like a veil. Brice watches her and I watch Brice. We're at his uncle's house. The backyard roof overhangs and I sit in the shade, disenchanted with swimming. The water is cold and there's a knot in my stomach, my throat. I don't know why except I don't like this boy—this Brice who seems to be my sister's boyfriend and who looks at her hungrily. He's only a year younger than I am, skinny and loud, foolishly confident, easy with opinion and insult—a spoiled brat. He gets what he wants and he clearly wants my sister. I think I might try to step in, build a wall around her, but when my sister looks up at him—his long, pale limbs, blondish hair, chlorine eyes—I see he already has her, or will soon. She flicks her hazel glances toward and away from him, as demure and savage as a hummingbird, and there's rawness about the way she moves, the way she splashes him, how she becomes suddenly hurt, badly hurt, if he teases her too much, how easily she forgives him. When did this happen?

It's August in the summer between my freshman and sophomore year of high school, and any authority I had over my little sister by virtue of age or experience is gone. She'd exceeded me in beauty long ago (our father sure to mention this at every opportunity), and here she is with this boy, and who am I to say what comes next? The only boy to claim me that way had left me bruised in a basement in Spokane—ridiculed me for not having fought him harder. No. I can only presume to know nothing. When my sister draws her attention away from Brice and toward me for a shining moment, she smiles and I smile back. Why show her what I'm thinking?

All the thoughts I have these days are poisonous. I know only this: no one should listen to me.

✳

Sunday in Barcelona—no one to speak to. The low throng of cathedral bells has knolled three times, but I'm weak, feverish, with blisters on my throat and have already walked down the six flights once before to buy water and try to make a phone call. There's no electricity in my apartment, and my eyes are too sensitive to read, so there's nothing to do but daze out the window, let the sun stretch its indirect light into my room. After a long while, I realize my eyes are focused on an old man who is sleeping. He lives in the building across from mine, but I'm farsighted and the alley between us is narrow enough for me to see him clearly. He has shucked his pale shirt and lies on his back on a single cot, his hands folded over his sunken belly—a tuft of white hair on his chest. The slack skin around his neck and jaw is yellow in the afternoon light; his black hair is thin and his wide mouth stays slightly open. If I squint, he almost looks like my grandfather—my mother's sweet dad—now many years in the earth. I witness the short rise and fall of his breath.

Earlier, I'd walked around the quiet streets—all the *mercados* barred shut, the people elsewhere—the gray stone buildings rising up around me, blocking out the light so that it was easy to imagine myself at the bottom of a deep ravine. I was looking for a phone booth at which I could make an international call, my calling card ready in my pocket. I wandered a long time before I made a good turn and the ravine opened up to a modest *plazuela*, lined with tender trees and with a phone booth at each corner. After several attempts, I got through to my mother's line, but no one was home—that lonely ringing. So, I went back to my small apartment and dragged a chair and a jug of water over to one of the windows where I still sit, occasionally sipping, wondering what the hell I'm doing here.

To learn Spanish, sure, but I could have taken classes in the States, gone into less debt, been less alone. I consider, for a moment, that I just like to travel, but something about this thought seems disingenuous. The sunlight makes my head ache, so I close my eyes, imagine myself in the backseat of a speeding car. The windows are rolled down so that the wind beats my face, my hair like a dark flag behind me, and in the front, Jasmine rides shotgun. Brice is driving without a license, headed north on I-5 in his mother's stolen car. The car is a manual and he's riding the clutch—the smell of smoldering newsprint wafts over us as he works his way through the gears. He'd driven six hours to take Jasmine from our aunt's house, where our mother had sent her to keep her away from Brice. It was a last-ditch effort to save her from their adolescent obsession, but he'd found her (his prized possession) and took her back.

But I wasn't there in the car with them. I don't know why this vision, which isn't from my life, comes back to me a decade later in Spain. I never imagined it in the months she was gone with Brice, our parents growing more and more hysterical. My sister came home a long time ago—is still there—why would it matter anymore? Six flights down, there are children running through the cobbled streets, kicking a ball between them. Their scuffles and hard breaths bounce off the pavement and rise up to me in echo. At the end of the street, another boy calls to the group and they call back in unison then run toward the voice, too far away for me to hear them anymore. The boys are probably the age of my nephews. I open my eyes briefly, then close them again, and in the flicker between, I see that the old man has curled over on his side, his long arms wrapped around his chest. Somewhere in the building, the next floor down, a woman sings from her window in the long lines of Arabic. I'd thought a trip to Spain alone might assuage my mind of the constant envy of elsewhere.

But it's the Fourth of July, and no one here knows what that means. On another continent, families are gathered in backyards, parks, camp grounds, slapping mosquitoes away from their arms, grilling meat and corn, drinking cold beer, eating ice cream, waiting for the sky to go dark. There are airplanes writing names in the sky, bees alighting on paper plates, wish-seeds floating into uncombed hair and the sugary surface of fried dough. And later, children making loops of light with sparklers, the shimmer of fireworks reflected on the hoods of cars, lovers hiding in fields of sweet-grass, sandy blankets rubbed with oil, dedications on the radio. I imagine my family together beneath the bright explosions, linking their hands—a gap where I'm not. I open my eyes.

Our mother was never still while Jasmine was gone. For months, she paced, cried, stared out the window, hung up *missing* posters—Jasmine's black-and-white face staring out of each telephone pole. Our mother emerged from her bedroom in the morning always with red, swollen eyes, the lines along her mouth growing deeper. Then she wandered through the rooms and the yard like *La Llorona*—no longer the mother I knew. She hired a detective with money our grandma gave her and whenever she wasn't working, she'd drive and drive and drive, chasing fog, the movements of small animals in grass, or else she'd weep into the phone, listening to who-ever claimed they knew how to bring her home. Her despair was complete and I knew better than to distract her from it. I tried to be helpful, good, and otherwise stayed out of her vigil. *Doesn't she know she's breaking my heart?*

I knew, also, to stay out of our father's way, which was easy, since he spent more and more time at the bars and when he came home he'd stum-ble and rant around the house, "The more you look, the more you look like a fool, Cecilia. We have three other kids—I mean, Jesus Christ, it's not like we don't have enough children without her. Jasmine wants to run away, let her." Or else he'd explain in avid detail to whoever would listen how he'd planned to kill Brice—a shovel to the head—and bury him in the founda-tion of a house he was working on.

A while later, when it was clear she wasn't returning, I'd helped our mother look for clues in Jasmine's room—a letter, a diary, anything that might lead us to her. Instead, we found her handmade boxes filled with animal bones. Because of Jasmine's gift for drawing, our mother encouraged her collection of potential figures, but her drawings had become increasingly dark, and this collection seemed to speak beyond art.

When I try to make a timeline of deaths and burials, I conclude that the first in her collection was her frog, who escaped from his aquarium and was found a week later, dried dead. I remember her holding his limp, green body in her palm, telling us to leave her alone. We left her alone as she cried in her room. As she cried, she folded a little box out of newspaper, tore a piece of fabric from her own blanket, wrapped him up like a bouquet, glued his six-inch casket shut, and placed him under her bed.

The second death must have been her rabbit, whose heart failed after a Rottweiler attack. A shoebox was decorated in her honor and placed in the garden to decompose. The whole family witnessed the burial. A long time later, she must have unearthed the bones, and again, placed them under her bed in a handmade box. There were the skeletons of birds she found half-dead on sidewalks, chicken bones, hamster bones, the skeleton of a fish. My mother and I stared at the contents of the boxes and each other as we pulled them out, one by one.

I hear a knock at the door and when I pull it open, the blond boy outside pushes me back and walks past me to the kitchen, sits at the table, smiling. It's Brice. Jasmine has been gone for months and though we knew he'd been hiding her, no one could prove it. Brice's mother was a tall, blond blank who, after her divorce, had indulged her son's every wish, and denied that my sister was living with her. My mother had sent police to their house, but Brice had hidden Jasmine so well (she was small—folded up on the top shelf of his closet) that they couldn't find her.

"Do you know where Jasmine is?" He grins. He must have been watching the house—my parents had just left—and he'd taken this opportunity to visit. He sits with his legs splayed, relaxed, an elbow on the table, and I feel a violent, dismaying rage welling up in my chest. Mileah, our eleven-year-old sister, hovers in the doorway with her wide green eyes, and our brother, Micah, paces the living room.

"Do you?" He tries again.

"No."

"I know."

"Did you come to tell us where she is?" Maybe they'd had a fight and she was coming home.

He lets out an exaggerated laugh, stands up for a moment to throw his hands in my face, "You don't know shit and I don't have to tell you shit." His smile widens. He sits back down.

"Tell me where she is." I consider going to the kitchen drawer where we keep the knives, but my feet stay planted. There's something about him that is disarmingly familiar. *She traded one tyrant for another*, I think.

"Okay . . ." he says, leaning forward conspiratorially, "She's . . ." I take a step toward him. He shoots back into the seat. "She's wherever I say she is, *bitch*. She's *mine*. I control her. She'll do whatever I want." I try to scream at him, but when I open my mouth, nothing comes out. Instead, my face trembles. I curl my hands into fists, but somehow I can't make my arms swing up to his face. While I stand there, completely ineffectual, he rises to his feet and walks toward the front door. Before he leaves the house he says, "I'm bored with you. You're fucking boring. And ugly. I'm gonna go see your sister now," then latches the door behind himself, softly.

It was my cue, but the spotlight wouldn't light up. The huge, hot machine had been temperamental since I took on the job, but now it simply wasn't working, and at such a pivotal scene—one of the few narrative scenes in *Babes in Toyland*. I was working a job each night after school for Portland's Musical Theatre Company, enduring each performance of the holiday favorite. The playwright and his librettist had composed the play as a studied attempt at another *Wizard of Oz*, but with more lavish spectacle and less storyline. Between rehearsals, nightly shows, and weekend matinees, I'd seen the musical at least twenty times, and although I had most of it memorized, I had no idea what it amounted to. It was a nightmarish mash of fairytale and nursery rhyme with elaborate costumes and shrill sopranos. I hadn't bothered to tell my friends at school I could get them free passes, and speaking to my family about anything other than my runaway sister was pointless—they no longer had use for details.

So that's what I kept close to me as I rode the humid city buses to and from work, rain pouring down in a kind of operatic drama, thankful for the brief reprieve from home. Because resources were limited, and I only worked the spotlight, the director thought it best to give me the headset without a working microphone, so during the malfunction—the voices of the actors rising from the stage without any light to guide them across—I could hear the director yelling, but couldn't respond.

Our parents had found Jasmine and dragged her home, but she wouldn't stay. I hadn't seen her, only heard her from an adjacent room. A guttural howl snapped me out of sleep and before I could fully untangle the nightmare I was having from my waking mind, I found myself pressed against the cool wall, my heart pounding, listening to the unrelenting voice in the next room wail itself hoarse. Jasmine's room had been vacant so long, I hadn't considered that she'd returned, and in my half sleep, believed a wolf or coyote was caught there—something primal and furious. She screamed in full force, kicking the walls, throwing any object she could land her hands on. It wasn't until I heard my mother's voice saying "Jasmine" in a silent space between fits that I understood my sister was in the house. But in the morning she was gone again, so was our father, and our mother's face was ashen over the kitchen table where she stared at the clean metal surface, too desperate to eat.

It was raining when I left for the bus stop that morning, and still raining on my dark, brisk walk from the high school to the theater. After the first few days at work, I'd realized it was better to stay in the empty hallways of my high school to wait for my evening shift rather than make the long ride home and back. I could do homework there without interruption, and it made me feel ghostly to roam the halls at night, peering into the empty classrooms. *If I were invisible, I could do what I wanted. I could walk right out of the city and never come back.* To keep warmth from escaping my body, I crossed my arms over my chest and walked faster, trying to imagine the tepid air of the high-ceilinged theater as a kind of reward for my arrival, and trying not to think of where Jasmine might be.

Spotlight! Spotlight! The director kept yelling, though I no longer had control. In the obscured scene, the sibling protagonists were traveling together through a haunted forest. They had run away from their murderous uncle and would soon arrive in Toyland, which they would find as dangerous as the house they had fled. Once there, they would have to disguise themselves as toys to survive, but in the forest they were openly lost, stumbling forward and forward, not knowing they were in the middle of losing themselves. I decided, as the director kept screaming, that I liked the scene better in blackout—none of the visual confusion that an excess of petticoats creates, none of the exaggeration of the doll-faced actors, just their voices calling out of the darkness toward the silent audience. They could have been anywhere.

Red earth, yellow earth, and pale beige seem to smear like paint as we drive past. Occasionally, a cluster of acacia or thorn shrubs splash the Kenyan landscape green, or way out on the plain, a cluster of white bones. The sky is a solid band of blue heat. Along the highway there are dry ditches where women with pitchers of water on their heads walk from what looks like nowhere to what looks like nowhere.

After a long while of driving we come to a makeshift market where a few vendors sit in the heat with their mounds of produce piled on collapsible tables. I notice one woman in particular, in a green and orange kanga, whose scarred cheeks reveal the gold beneath her deep, brown skin. When I walk past, she stands up, lifts two sweet limes from her table, and holds them out to me, balancing them on her wide palm as if they were chosen together—a necessary pair pulled from the waxen masses. And because I'm a romantic, I buy them—walk a while down the dusty road where I find the slim shade of an acacia, and stand there peeling the fruit, scraping my teeth along the white, inner rind, pressing my fingers into the seams of the pale yellow wedges to pull them apart, eat them slowly—water, bitter, sweet. I'm trying to believe I'm in Kenya. It seems so unlikely. The ship on which I arrived wasn't scheduled for a stay on the African continent except for a few days in Egypt, but while we were a day's travel from Cairo's port city, we heard from the crew that the USS Cole was bombed near Yemen and the captain had decided not to take us through the Suez Canal. He changed course to a route around the Cape of Good Hope, with a port stop in Kenya.

Even as I stand here in the dust of the country, I realize I'm incapable of seeing it. Layered over everything I encounter is an image I used to keep in my mind; just after Jasmine returned, before our father left, I used to lie in bed at night in my thin-walled attic room thinking of the Kenyan savannahs I'd seen on PBS. It was the coldest December on record, the furnace was broken, and my father had refused to fix it or allow my mother to pay to have it fixed. The temperatures dropped and the wind rose. He was in a manic phase—swollen-loud and drunk—and my mother was refusing to sleep with him: "If you kids are cold, you can blame it on your mother. She's my wife goddamnit, and if she doesn't give me what I want, then why the hell should I give her what she wants?" Our mother, beneath her dark curtain of hair, cried in the kitchen, shivering.

Then the water heater broke, and he refused to fix this as well. He took his showers and slept elsewhere, only coming home briefly from the bars to taunt us: "It sure is cold in here. And not even a hot shower to take in the morning." We didn't know where he spent his nights. No heat and no hot water—no reprieve from the cold. He'd been threatening to leave for good and she believed he meant it this time, so she waited.

For the first few nights, the walls slanted down over me while I shook.

Instead of sleeping, I thought of Jasmine in the next room, wondered what she was thinking. She'd returned just in time to watch our parents' marriage dissolve. She was gone and gone and then she was there again, sleeping in the room we'd shared as children. But it was clear she no longer accepted her role in the family, and I didn't know how to regard her. Her homecoming was followed by a kind of amnesia—no one spoke of what had occurred in the months before. They told her she could date Brice if she wanted, and she would begin school again as soon as possible. Brice occasionally came by the house, arriving without apology. Everything, it seemed, had already been forgiven. I fell into orbit around her, afraid she might leave again, imagining the tumult it would cause.

For four nights, I watched frost spread slowly across my window until all I could see was crystal-white over blackness—not even smoke from the chimney next door, just the way the frost shimmered when the window rattled from the wind. I watched my breath roll out in front of me, as heavy and tangible as fruit. One night, delirious maybe, I tried to envision my breath as actual fruit, ripe in the sun. Then I imagined the sun itself. Beneath the sun was a wide savannah of tall grass and acacia trees—among the trees, lions through with their hunt, light pooling in the open muscles of their kill.

I'd seen it in documentaries through the static of our television, pressed my nose practically to the screen to watch the zebras, the wildebeests, the Masai in their red robes walking barefoot and certain, never looking down. I began to take in these shapes, swallowing them, letting them become part of my body so that each night I went to sleep with an African sun in my chest, huge and red on the horizon of my ribs, always setting, never going out.

I can't remember how I arrived. Staring up into the darkness, I begin to see the vague shapes of people in tiered seats. They shift and breathe lightly, though altogether their breath has made the room heavy, humid, and the bright lights above me, shining directly into my face, away from the dark crowd, make the heat worse. My face feels waxy, itches, and when I scratch it, my nails come back with thick make-up beneath them. *Strange. This must be a dream.* When I look down, I realize I'm standing on the edge of a painted stage. *Why are all these people looking at me?* I try to retrace where I was before this moment, and can only recall my father as he left the house—"You'll all beg me to come back." That was in December. *What month are we in now?*

She left without me—without even telling me she was leaving. How much time have I spent imagining our breakout together, and she just drops from her window one night? Something like jealousy lights up in my mind. I was too pragmatic to jump on impulse, always imagined us starving, roaming the streets, and decided, the way our mother must have decided so many times, that waiting is best. I flinched. I made excuses for his violence until it had gone so far beyond acceptable that I no longer remembered what I was waiting for. I stopped asking what was tolerable. I stopped getting in his way.

Then she left.

Then she returned, but my mind was already mired. To ask her how she felt—to say how I felt—seemed an absurd and exhausting chore, one I refused. My body floated through the days, performing the tasks I assigned it, and soon I was convinced it was all an act; I learned how to perform myself.

Two figures stand behind me to my left, and when I look over, I almost laugh. One is dressed as a pauper and one is dressed as a witch (a terrible wig and fake nose curling off the witch's real nose). They look at me intensely. I recognize their faces—two friends from my theater class—and realize we're in the middle of a performance—*a dress rehearsal?* I assess the crowd again. *No. It's a full house.*

I remember now: Jasmine's home, our father's gone, and I'm playing The Baker's Wife in the school musical. It's opening night of *Into the Woods*. No one in the family could come. We're still in the first act and my character has gone into the dreaded forest to find the items she needs to lift a curse from her family. While I was dressing backstage I began crying for no reason—kept crying and crying and reapplying my makeup, and was still crying as I stood behind the curtain, then just before my first sung line—"I wish"—I stopped and stepped onto the stage. This is not, as it turns out, a dream. Everyone is looking directly at me. It's my line, but I don't remember what to say. I wish someone would turn out the lights.

❋

Jasmine and I have walked away from the market, and sit at a nearby restaurant, our aunt leaning toward us over the dark, glossy table, expectant. She's just laid out the problem between us and now it's our turn to talk. But we haven't spoken much in the three years since her wedding, barely spoke before, and it's difficult to begin now that the silence has lived so long with us. The waiter comes by to take our order, and though he stands at my back, I hear his voice shift when he sees us and becomes uncertain—he's clearly interrupting. My aunt orders a pinot grigio. I order a Cabernet. My sister orders nothing, is as still and closed as a mollusk beside me. In my peripheral view, I see her head slightly bowed. I'm staring at the mahogany woodwork between window panes, then past it to the narrow, downtown alley where a skinny white boy in tie-dye and dreads is walking down the street, tossing up a single bowling pin as he goes—the heavy twirl of it.

The waiter returns with our drinks, naming them as he sets them in front of us, "Pinot grigio, Cabernet, water." I feel like bolting out of the restaurant, running and running until everything is too far away to see. "Anything else for you ladies right now?" the waiter offers, trying to be courteous, but quick.

"No, thank you. We're fine," our aunt offers, brushing her curly hair away from her face. She's chair of the board at this meeting of three. Jasmine and I are going to make amends, she's decided, and I'm grateful to her for her intervention—but confrontation of this magnitude makes me nauseous, and my sister's perpetual silence wracks me. I want something new with her, but don't know how to begin.

Earlier, I saw her in profile as I approached the market and was struck by how happy she looked. Her tanned face and arms were illuminated by the afternoon light. She wore a sleeveless shirt and paint-splattered jeans—held a paintbrush firmly in one hand, giving her full attention to a canvas she'd duct-taped to the brick wall near her booth. As I approached her, I began to see the canvas more clearly: a leafless tree twisting over the edge of a deep ravine, and in the ravine, a pale moon buoyed up by darkness. She stretched her lean body to brush a small detail at the top of the canvas as her husband—tall, wavy brown hair, handsome cheekbones—watched her hands move.

In my mind, she's always been an artist, but it took her years of tenacity to gain momentum in Portland's art scene, and now she goes to the downtown market every weekend to paint and sell her work. Her husband and daughter always accompany her while their sons—now teenagers—stay home. I've been kept familiar with her progress from our mother and little sister, and called to congratulate her a few times, but have always been greeted politely by her voicemail message, and my calls have never been returned.

A few pedestrians stopped to watch her work and ask questions. She turned around to answer them. Her daughter ran into the scene, laughing and stopping with a little jump at the edge of Jasmine's tarp. While still in conversation with the strangers, Jasmine lifted an arm so that her daughter could slide closer, wrap her skinny arms around her waist and squeeze tight. In a smiling response to the strangers and her daughter, she made a long gesture in the air with her paintbrush hand and lowered her free hand to rest on her daughter's head. Her girl, Elexis, has dark, almost black hair and my sister's childhood face. I've been gone so long, I hardly know Jasmine's children anymore, but when Elexis appeared in the scene, I wanted very much to run up and spin her around as I used to when she was very little—but I didn't want to startle her, so I approached slowly.

I take a sip of Cabernet, worry it on my tongue, press my forefinger to the base of the glass to see my faint print remain. I try to bring up her wedding, but she shakes her head, says, "It's not about the wedding." *Yes, of course not,* I think. *It was never about the wedding.* Our growing apart was largely unconscious and happened over years—fissures spreading through the foundation until the house fell finally down.

When we were children, our mother worked nights at a restaurant, and I was left in charge—her surrogate. I tried to stand, as our mother stood, between our father's violent temper and my siblings. Those were the years the nightmares arrived, for which I eventually stopped sleeping. It's been over a decade since I left, and still every night that I manage to fall asleep I dream I'm in our childhood house, our father always hovering in threat. I was never able to stop him—not even once—and the braver I stood, the more enraged he became. Failing and failing, I came to understand what Jasmine seemed to know all along—the only triumph we could hope for was escape.

All through the Wisconsin winter, I watched the lake for signs. It seemed impossible to me that such a large body of water might turn solid enough to walk on, though everyone told me it would, and from the window of my high English Department office, I monitored the steady growth of the white shore as it stretched in toward the blue heart of Lake Mendota. Walking to and from the university from the bus stop, I marveled at the visual decadence of my breath, how the vigorous cold stung my lungs and was almost a persuasive force against my warm body—*go back inside.* Still, I loved to stroll along the bright frivolities displayed in the shop windows along State Street—paper lanterns, clothing, beads, brass statues, incense, coffee—and to imagine the places I'd take my sisters if they were able to visit, though I knew they'd never come.

Jasmine and I hadn't spoken since her wedding in June. I'd called and called to ask what I'd done to make her so angry, but she wouldn't call back. At night, I'd lay awake going over every moment, staring into the dim whiteness of my bedroom ceiling, becoming alternately angry and sad, occasionally waking Chris with my restlessness. Chris and I had moved to Madison together and were trying for the first time to make a go of domestic bliss, which was more difficult than either of us had expected. Still, he was kind each time I accidentally woke him, turning his face toward me in the dark and throwing a long arm across my body, saying sleepily, "Thinking about your sister again?"

"Yeah. Sorry to wake you."

"It's okay, but there's nothing you can do about it right now. Try, at least, to rest."

The freeze deepened, thwarting any possibility of snowmelt, and I didn't go home that Christmas—the plane ticket was expensive, and what was the point of going into more debt if I wasn't welcome? Our student loan debt, all the traveling I'd done before, and our move from Virginia to Wisconsin added up to a pile of bills as hefty as the snowdrifts. I tried to quell my wanderlust by eating curry, watching travel shows, and paying for the places I'd already been.

Instead of traveling, Chris worked on his graduate school applications—it was likely we'd be moving again in the summer—and I sulked around our small tinseled tree unless friends came by to visit. Lying in the dark, listening to the cold bedroom windows rattle, I'd sometimes think of those days just before our father left—how Jasmine must have shivered in the room next to mine, though I never thought to visit her, and she never thought to visit me. To ward off the cold, I'd try to conjure my Kenyan savannahs, but could no longer feel them in my body.

One evening, tired of trying to sleep, I suited up to go the edge of the lake nearest our apartment, walked the mere block to the shore's edge, barely distinguishable from the lake itself—everything white. While I stood there staring into the minimalist landscape, I saw two forms way out toward the center of the lake scurrying across the ice. No human figure accompanied them, and as I watched the forms weaving back and forth across each other's paths, crouched low, I realized the forms were wild—coyotes, or feral dogs running together across the ice.

By June, it'd been a year since my sister's silence began, and the lake was through aching over its shores. The floods had come and gone and the stink they'd brought had abated into the lake's usual slight scent of mud and fish. Along the lake near our apartment was a bike path that I liked to ride in the early evenings after dinner, before sunset. I'd get on my hefty mountain bike and pedal through the neighborhood to the smooth, pale pavement arching with the shore of Lake Monona.

The path led around part of the lake and through Olin Park, where there were always people playing soccer on the fields—and past the park to the railroad tracks that led to a tunnel beneath the freeway, then away from the freeway onto a wide road lined with astonishingly tall goldenrod and prairie grass, always rabbits or squirrels running into the brush, and along that road the electrical plant, and past the electrical plant, the sewage treatment plant, where I tried my best to pedal and hold my breath, but always lost from laughing just before the sharp turn onto the narrow highway along the marshland preserve, where a fresh wind always saved me, and a single wooden-plank trail stretched out over the swaying foxtails, until finally reaching the part of the path exclusive for cyclists and pedestrians, the road framed on either side by fields of midwestern foliage: honeysuckle, bindweed, yellow star thistle, purple loosestrife, the lace of wild parsnip, small stands of pine and black alder, and woven everywhere throughout the fields, the triumphant applause of goldenrod.

Like all places with long winters, Madison's summers seem framed in endless light, and along these fields that light was amplified. By the time I reached the pedestrian road, my legs were rubbery with exhaustion, and a slick sweat covered me, dripping salt into my eyes. Perhaps it was the delirium of strenuous work, or the feeling of my body moving so swiftly and perpetually forward, or how the road stretched out so straight for so long that I wanted to give myself to it, but I was always moved to close my eyes for a moment or two—let the heavy machine beneath me whir forward without my help and feel the wind I was creating. In that blindness, drawn into the confusion of not knowing what was ahead, I always felt a little tug at the center of my chest like an illness, or a call to prayer. Caught up in the scent of earth and grass, the vibration of wheels against the road—breathless, exhausted, in danger of crashing—I could almost believe it led home.

A dark figure grabs my shoulder to shake me awake, saying my name. Once my eyes focus, I realize it's the shape of my mother, her voice unusually urgent.

"Do you know where Jasmine is?"

I pause. "In her bed?"

"No. She's not there. Did you hear that thump?"

"I've been sleeping."

My mother sits up straight, forces calm into her voice.

"She's not downstairs, or outside . . . Do you know where she might have gone?"

"What time is it?"

"Two a.m."

"I don't know . . . Beach School? Maybe she couldn't sleep."

"Why would she go to Beach if she couldn't sleep?"

"I don't know," I lied.

"Will you help me find her?"

"Yeah, let me get dressed."

We go downstairs and out the front door to my mother's small, blue car. Beneath the streetlights, moisture rises from the pavement like smoke. An early rain makes the air feel raw. I sit on the passenger's side, breathing in the ghost of summer rain while we weave in and out of empty streets. An hour passes at this venture, and nothing. This was the first time she ran away, at twelve years old. I'm a melancholy fifteen, and don't believe she could be in any danger.

"Why would she leave like that?"

"I don't know."

"Did she say anything to you?"

"We haven't spoken much lately," I yawned. "Maybe she's home by now."

"I need your help, Danielle."

"Okay," I shake myself up, "Try just going straight down Concord." She does.

"Wait! What was that?"

"Where?"

"I saw someone go behind that truck."

"Are you sure? Did it look like Jasmine?"

"Yeah, pull over."

She pulls over. I run across the street toward the streak of dark gold hair that briefly flashed, then disappeared. Jasmine scurries into the corner of a driveway, into thin bushes.

"Jasmine." Just wind and distant traffic. "I can see you, Jasmine, just come out." I approach the bushes slowly. When I reach the bushes I crouch down, see patches of her face through the leaves.

"What are you doing, Jazz? Mom and I have been looking for you. It's late." She breathes hard.

I pull back a branch where her eyes shine, darker than they should be. "Why aren't you talking to me?" Silence. A car passes. Its headlights light her face for a moment, then leave it dark again.

"What's going on, Jazz? Mom and I are both really worried about you . . ." She jumps out of the bushes and tries to run past me, but I catch her by the crook of her arm. She scratches and twists, growling until I let her go. When she's a few feet away from me she stops, looks down at the pavement. "God, Jazz, will you let me take you home? You're being crazy." Our mom approaches the curb in her blue car, and leans over to open the passenger-side door. It swings open easily.

"Hi, Jazzy. It's cold out here. Why don't you come home," Mom says.

Jasmine glares at us, then looks over her shoulder—to what? Someone waiting for her? Did the darkness reach up to run its fingers through her hair?

"Yeah, it's cold," I agree. "It's dangerous."

"Where?" Jasmine asks.

"What do you mean . . . right here . . . now . . . where we are . . ."

She floats past me to the front passenger seat and waits until I'm slumped in the back before she says, "You're wrong."

"About what?" I ask, but she never answers.

Begin in December with an ache in your shoulders—the moment you stand in the open doorway and announce that you are leaving. No one is asking you to stay. All of them wear the same strange expression and you can't tell what it means. A little ice settles in your stomach. There's a sudden dullness in your head. Maybe it's just the booze. The tightness in your shoulders moves up to the foothills of your neck and there's a small twinge in your top vertebrae as you turn away from the door, their faces, and stride across the yard, fists ready though there's nothing to slam—relief? Was it relief? The cold air arrives in gales, bitter across your face. You have a hazy memory of weathermen on the news talking of northern fronts and high pressures that keep out the blanketing clouds. The sky high—cold and blue—no moisture gathering—a direct and open field to the atmosphere.

It's a week before Christmas and there's not enough whiskey in the world to make you feel right. For too long, you've watched your wife and children turn away. Nothing seems to make up for whatever you've done and you can't stand to see them anymore—all blaming eyes. After everything you've done. After you kicked cocaine. After you watched the future you imagined for yourself splinter and drop into dust. After you worked, soaked through in the blinding rain and broiled in the sun, season after season, hammering down your bones, writing their names on the bare insides of walls, stairways, elevator shafts like secret love letters—how can they look at you that way as you're leaving? How can they stare at you and not ask you to stay? You've got lead in your blood and needles in your spine and the only thing that assuages your constant pain is a good, deep drunk.

You peel out of the icy drive toward the Ninth Street house where all of your children were born, were you all used to live together, and where you lived alone before the children, before you met Cecilia, began this whole mess. You peel out of the drive, letting them know how quickly you want out. *Not one more goddamned minute*, you hear yourself say as you turn the corner, out of their sight. But by the time you get to Prescott, you're driving slowly and your stomach feels raw. *How could they be so ungrateful?*

The neighborhood is changing, but people still avoid this part of the city, with its threatening graffiti, broken and boarded-up windows, shattered bottles, and grease on the sidewalks. More than the terrain, it's the faces of the people who live here—mostly black—who know exactly what they don't have and are weary from having never known better. *So what.* No one ever did you any favors, either, and you aren't afraid of a few punk kids, a few sad mothers and their missing men.

It's hard to find renters in this part of town and the house is empty except for a fine film of dust. The furnace is broken, the electricity is off, and the pipes are busted, though you don't know this yet. You walk through the dark to the small bundle of firewood the last renters left and open the black woodstove to light a fire. While you fumble with the matches you're surprised to find yourself crying. You feel sorry. You feel so fucking sorry and you don't even know why. The fire catches. You close the door to the woodstove to let the black cast iron radiate. The floor is dead cold and you roll out a thin sleeping bag, your eyes swollen and wet, your head pounding, the high ceiling looming over you, and the leaves from the holly outside scratching at the windows—curtainless, smeared with fingerprints.

You can't go back now. You can't go back on what you said. No pillow—
you roll up your jacket and lay your head on the hard, dark mound, shivering, delirious, half-dreaming of light.

It's cut with sugar. It's cut with cornstarch, talc, lactose, tetracaine, pro-
caine, lidocaine. It's cut with heroin, PCP, LSD, caffeine, amphetamine,
hashish. It's a shit cut. Maybe no coke in it at all. Maybe do another line
to be sure. You're not getting the high the high the high; you're not a hur-
ricane. You look around for the john, but now you're not in the club—no
glitter in your pockets. There you're brilliant and no one can touch you—
never tired, never hungry, you spin the room. You spin in the room. How
did you get here—the long mirrors and mauve wallpaper—how did you
get back home? At the club you're pure, from superior stock, everyone else
is cut with shit. That's why they want you out, way out; they're so jealous
they'll drop your body in the river. Like that guy they found. You knew
that guy. That guy worked for you—what was his name? But you're smarter
than him. His bloody, stupid, swollen face. You press the barrel of the gun
to your face—the metal not even cool anymore you've been holding it so
long. All warmed up. You and your gun are all warmed up and you can
hear the bosses outside your windows—the high-up bosses, the ones you
haven't met, whose names you don't know. Fucking idiots think you can't
hear them. You can hear their rubber heels on the pavement, a throat
clearing, the hammer of a gun clicking back, moths beating at the back
porch light, the water in the Willamette rushing downstream, miles away,
a woman laughing. Any minute they'll crash through—try to steal your
money, your wife, your coke, but you have it covered. You can see them
coming. In your mind. In your pure mind.

But Cecilia might ruin it, might give you away. *Cecilia, Cecilia, you're
breaking my heart.* She's sitting up looking at you with her eyes wide—you
can see it in the dark—like she's going to say something. *Shut up. Shut
the fuck up. Don't say a thing or we'll all be dead,* you think, and point the

gun at her head so she knows to be quiet. Bundle of money and coke you squat over like a golden egg. They think you'll be in the bed with your wife, but you're in the middle of the room, crouched on the carpet and Cecilia's got those scared eyes sitting up in the bed, the blankets pulled up to her chest like she doesn't know what's going on. Like she never expected this— why the fuck would you sell coke in the first place? Always broke, always working—too many kids and three fucking jobs and can't make enough. Any minute, they'll break through and she'll see what you're into—so high up now they want you dead. These are the consequences. Had to do it. Had to do it. Should have never had kids. Should have never left the mountain. Thought the money would shut her up, but now she's always worried, scared. Worse than before—keeps asking you to stop, keeps saying she never wanted you to. She wanted it. She didn't know she wanted it, but she did, and now this is where you've come to. Her big green eyes light up and quiver in the dark. They make you nauseous. They make you tremor and sweat. You can hear her breathing, the tension in her throat, how she's trying not to cry. Another boss is thinking outside the window—you can hear the neurons inside his skull like fireworks—he's given the go-ahead. You can feel his nod. He's ready to pounce. Your muscles twitch. The room spins. You wait for the crash. You wait for the crash. You wait for the crash.

Someone once told you that when the moon is directly overhead, you weigh slightly less, and that seems true tonight. It floats above you, tugging at your body, illuminating the sharp slope and subalpine meadow. Summer and you are in love with wild peony, northern starflowers, early blue violets, blue-eyed grass, elk weed, huckleberry, skyrocket gilia, pine, dandelion, clover, and sorrel. You've smoked some green and have lifted into a blissful high, your body like a swift cloud over the moonlit mountainside—running up and down, up and down. Just you and the coyotes howling at the moon. The wild night sky fills you and you become part of its tireless beauty. You don't hurt anymore. A euphoric sense of certainty has awakened in you and it fuels your body, your mind—you could run all night on moonlight and wild berries. Whatever vexed you before, whatever restless ghost provoked you into choosing the sleepwalk you lived in the valley, is gone. You're learning to sew, forage for plants, catch and cook your own food, and you feel good at the simple self-sufficiency of living. You think often of your kind grandfather, who taught you to fish, tie a good knot, light a fire. You like to imagine him steering his small metal boat through the sky.

Downstream, a loose commune has gathered. You like to visit and you like to leave. You live apart from them in the round house you made from poles and canvas—a smoke flap at the apex to keep a fire inside—warmth, cooked food. You keep to yourself for long throws, but each time you walk downstream you see something striking. A woman who arrived to the commune swollen bellied gave birth to a boy at night. Her man threw the afterbirth on the hillside for the coyotes to eat. Yesterday, you met a newcomer who breastfed a litter of kittens. The mother cat had died, and the woman cried as she let the mewling calico babies crawl over her large, bare breasts. You wanted to ask where her own baby was, but the fever of her tears made you turn away.

Walking for miles each day up flowered hills, through brush, beneath great pines, you're beginning to think of the children you'll have someday. You think of how you could live like this with a family—free from material ambition—live away from the city on some small plot of land, learn to farm. You don't have to be a torn-down suburban blank like your mother and stepfather. You don't have to go crazy like your father with his money lust, his prescription drugs, his shock therapy. You can see how your family will adore you, listen to you, like your sisters—you are a natural protector, a natural father. You feel—you have *always felt*—your physical and mental superiority among men and this is the era of imagining, of making what you imagine possible, and the shape of a new way of living rises before you as you grow closer and closer to the mountain. In spring, the low call of the birds in the trees unlocks something in your mind. You decide one morning while walking through a hushed field of orange jewelweed, you'll marry soon.

You wake on your hardwood bedroom floor, your head swimming all over the room. There's a woman in your bed whose face you don't know. She's long-limbed and fair, in a short, yellow dress, and lying in her vomit on your pillow. You get up slowly, and the dull glaze of spring light reflecting off the floor makes your head pound as you approach the young woman slowly, check her pulse. She's alive, so you leave her to sleep it off and walk slowly into your living room, where people from last night's party are still strewn around like dirty laundry. They're greasy, unconscious, with ashen faces, their party clothes stained. Two have pissed themselves. A big guy with a brown moustache and blue paisley shirt has smashed your coffee table with the weight of his body and is still lying there in the pieces. A teenage girl has torn down your living room curtains and rolled herself in them to keep warm. Her bare feet are dirty. Mescaline, opium, pot, acid, booze, whatever. Last night was supposed to be a good time. You've been working construction to have your own place, have some spending money, but who are these people? Cigarette burns in the arms of the couch and a few in the arms of the girl lying on the couch. To disrespect you that way—you feel sick, pit of your stomach sick, more than just nausea.

You consider waking everyone to throw them out, but imagine yourself cleaning all day. You think it best to wait until they wake, get some to help. Your front door is wide open. When you try to shut the door, you accidentally knock the ankle of a man splayed on the floor. He jerks up with an ugly expression, eyes barely opened, tells you to "fuck off," then lies back down. You're insulted, but don't feel like fighting.

You need food, coffee. Maybe you'll go get breakfast and see who's left to help clean when you get back. You step over the prone man to the threshold of the open door and into your yard, where you stare a long while at the empty space in the driveway where you always park your car. Your head feels like it's going to split open. You walk back inside and go to the kitchen for some aspirin and a glass of water. There's not a clean glass in the house, so you cup your hands over the filthy sink beneath the running faucet and drink, pop aspirin in your mouth, then drink again. The water is cool and clean on your palms and you stand there watching it pour over them, thinking of how long it's been since you've been down to the river or up to the mountain. *Fuck it.*

Maybe you say this out loud, maybe you only say it in your head, but each time you tell this story, this is the turning point: *Fuck it. Fuck this place*, you think, *Fuck work. Fuck rent. Fuck the parties. Fuck these people. I'm going to live in the mountains.*

You walk back into your bedroom, where the woman doesn't stir, grab a backpack, and walk around the house stuffing into it what you might need: boxers, socks, an extra pair of jeans, peanut butter, plastic tarp, hammer, matches. You roll up a sleeping bag, grab a skillet and saucepan from the cupboard, and tie them to the pack. In the basement, you find your tent, your dusty camping stove, fishing rod, and stainless steel cups. The last thing you grab is your guitar. When you walk through the living room on your way out, a disheveled blond woman is awake, sitting on the couch. She says, "Where are you going with all that stuff?"

"Does it matter to you?"

She thinks about this for a moment. "No, I guess not," and slumps into the cushions of the couch.

You step over the body of the sleeping man as you walk out of the house, down the steps, down the street to the nearest intersection, where you stick out a thumb. A tanned, long-haired couple in a beat-up station wagon stops. They're headed to Mount Hood and can take you the whole way. A year will pass before you're in the valley again.

An acrid breeze blows through the neighbors' slatted shed, becoming cooler and cooler until the blazing temperature calms into night's autumn-like sadness. You are fifteen and miserable, but won't give your stepfather the satisfaction of returning. During tonight's fight in the yard, you'd picked up the hedge trimmer and swung it at him in a fierce, screaming rage, and you saw in that moment in his face a real fear of you, and it made you feel righteous in your anger. You've ridden away on your bike, like a man. Who was he, anyway? Not your *real* father. Your real father wouldn't have second-guessed you. Through the slats, you watch a harem of trees, their elegant bodies veiled in starlight. The bones of the fried chicken your younger sister brought you for dinner still fill the small space with the scent of meat. You aren't sure how she found you, but felt tenderly toward her when she arrived with leftovers she'd stolen from the fridge and wrapped in a cloth napkin—her mess of curly hair, her large blue eyes full of concern. It was her father you'd been fighting, and she just wants you to love each other—thinks if she loves you double you'll come home.

Maybe I'll never go back, you think, folding your arms across your chest. It's 1968, and your older sister is in love. Your parents have been trying to keep her from it. When she left the house to live with your real father, who let her see her boyfriend, there was a bitter fight. "Whore," they called as she was leaving, lighting a white flame inside you. You thought of when you were children together—the stepchildren of the house—how you used to stay up late at night talking. She'd sneak into your room when she had nightmares. You liked that she wanted your protection. You'd stay awake with your rubber-band gun—*Don't worry, Vicki. If anyone tries to hurt you, I'll shoot them in the eye.*

She wasn't allowed to sleep in your room, so as soon as the sun began its campaign through your curtains, you'd wake her. On the way out she'd kiss your forehead and call you her hero. Your mother has never called you her hero, and your stepfather always looms in his plaid work shirt and worn jeans, belt in hand, his blue eyes flickering out of his darkly tanned face. They don't speak to you much anymore, except to criticize. *You're just like your father*, your mother keeps saying like a curse every time she is displeased with you. And how would you know what he's like to her? She doesn't have much to say about him. What you know you've overheard, or inferred from conversation.

It was bad between them—you're no fool. You're smarter than most, in fact, handsome, charming, and your father has explained that you don't have to listen to your stepfather because you come from superior stock. He's indulgent with himself, high-spirited and moody—disappears for long stretches of time and returns with holes in his memory. *Must have had a good time—can't remember a thing.* Sometimes when he's drunk, he tells you stories about his life, all twisted and strange: his mother's depression, her mania and visits to the hospital, as well as his own visits to the hospital. *E-lec-tro-con-vul-sive* therapy. The word rings through you. You wonder how it works. What it does to the mind. How it feels when the brain broils beneath conductive jelly. Who knows whose memories he's telling?

Since you were eleven, he's let you drive his car and likes to go on long drives with you, crossing and recrossing the city's many bridges. You like that Portland is strung with long, proud bridges, the smell of the Northwest waterways—clay, moss, rinsed fish, musk of gasoline, the faint smell of sawdust. Your favorite is the St. John's Bridge, its towers rising up like a gothic cathedral, its long, green body suspended over the Willamette. Each time you drive over together, your father declares the same fact: "Two of us have jumped off this bridge," one of them, his father. He doesn't tell you this to scare you. He likes to mention it as an interesting part of family history. From his stories it seems the men in your family only die from suicide— a bridge jumper, a hangman, a gunshot to the head—his voice swelling up with a kind of pride about it, a mixture of warmth and fascination. It makes the bridge mysterious, haunted. Each time you drive over it, you envision a man who looks like your father climbing the green suspension cables that form the bridge's ribs, balancing for a moment with his arms outstretched, then letting gravity pull him gracefully, unflinchingly to his death. You could almost applaud.

You clap your hands together in the drafty shed, trying to warm them a little. Why did your stepfather call you out into the yard? It seems to be happening more and more often—anger surging like a crowd in your mind, then scattering just as quickly. Sometimes you itch with wanting, restlessness, can feel it creeping up your spine. But your moods match the emotional tides of the day. You've seen the riots on the television, in the newspapers, in the voices and faces of other people, and you feel them in your body, your new ways of thinking. Things are changing and you can't explain it, don't want to. All your friends at school are enthralled by your ceaseless energy, the bright flame of you. Only your parents seem to dissent, and who are they to give advice? Look at their lives.

It seems they want you to leave, have been waiting for years. *We'd all be happier if I didn't go back.* There's still some summer in the air, but there's a powerful chill beneath it. You lean against the cool, splintered corner of the shed with the cloth napkin in your hands, contemplating your dinner of scraps.

*

It's summer again and you wake in the dark. Down the hall you hear a man's voice, and though you know it's your father's voice, it's unfamiliar. You haven't known him long. He shares the same name with your friend's father, so when your mother and stepfather asked if you wanted to stay the night at his house, you thought of the wrong man. You said yes, without hesitation, and as you ran to your room to stuff pajamas in a paper sack, you noticed your mother's sad, narrow face, the creases above her thin browns, the pull at the corners of her mouth. Even her wild, curly hair seemed weighted down as your stepfather drew near her, placed his hand on her back. It wasn't until the man arrived on your porch to take you away that you realized your mistake.

You've met your father once before, but when he showed up abruptly, after years of absence, and knocked on your family's latched screen door, your mother started yelling, made him stand there on the porch, and your stepfather stood protectively behind her. You were eleven years old and had known all your life that you had another father somewhere, a man whose face you shared, but you couldn't remember ever having known him. Because she feared the neighbors would whisper, she finally let him into the house. The stranger glided past her, sat down at the kitchen table, smiling wide at the scene he'd created. He addressed you and your older sister with ease, announced himself as your *real* father. Your stepfather bristled, but he was never one to make a scene, just stared at him carefully, his blue eyes flashing. The stranger at the table had straight white teeth that shone over every word. "Maybe you could come visit me sometime."

Your mother asked you and your sisters to go play elsewhere, which was fine by you. You were confused by the scene, how upset your mother was, and now that you're in your strange father's house, you're beginning to understand why. His laugh, echoing from the end of the hallway, stretches through the gloaming toward you. You get up from the bed, confused by the blackness—why are you waking in the dark?—and follow his voice down to the kitchen where you find him playing cards with a woman you haven't met. There's a bottle of gin, mostly gone, on the flecked metal table. Her sheer beige dress is loose in the collar and slips down to expose her pale, tender shoulder, the strap of her slip. You stare at her. Her red lipstick is smeared and her eyelids are heavy. She laughs when she sees you, says, "Look, he's up!"

She reaches out her hand to run her slim fingers through your curly hair, says, "He looks just like you," then turns her attention to the cigarette pack on the table, and asks vaguely as she pulls out a smoke, "Why'd he sleep so long, anyway? You sick, hon?"

You hadn't considered this before. You're dizzy, weak, a little nauseous—maybe you *are* sick.

"I crushed up some benzos and put them in his orange juice," your father says without looking up from his cards.

"You did what?!" Her voice is more amused than shocked and her tongue is slow.

"The damn kid was running around at 5 a.m. I had a hangover. He needed to shut up a while."

"How much did you give him?"

"Listen kid," he says, turning his broad face toward you, "When I was a boy and wouldn't shut up, they used to hit me over the head with a mallet." He says it deadpan. "Consider yourself lucky."

You think about your stomach, how empty it feels. You haven't eaten since dinner last night. You feel sick and you want to go home to your mother, who will give you soup, unfold your pajamas and lay them out on your bed, press her palm to your forehead to check for fever. There's a flood against your throat, but you don't let yourself cry. A box of cereal balances on the edge of the counter and you walk over to pick it up, then go to the fridge—no milk. Already, you are drifting down the hall with your box of cereal, away from your father and the woman whose knee he touches beneath the table, beneath her dress, his smile wide as a cat's. When you reach the room, you eat a few fistfuls in the dark, then crawl into bed, silent, your small, lean body spiraling in on itself—a little caterpillar. Listen—

I don't want this for you.

I want a different ending. All of this is half-truth anyway—strung together from nights you actually came home, slumped down at the kitchen table, then slurred at me for hours. Fourteen years and your stories still shift like a tidal net: sometimes you wake and the woman isn't there, sometimes it's him drawn under by the pills, sometimes *your* head is struck by the mallet . . .

Your father is kissing the strange woman now, moving his mouth down the front of her dress. You're closing your eyes, trying to shut out the light from the hallway, the shadow of branches from the tree outside. Ghost of a daughter, I'll float into the room. When I kneel down, throw your arms around my neck. I'll lead us down the hall, past the kitchen with its bad light and gin. The man and the woman will keep laughing and drinking, drinking and laughing so hard, they won't even notice us leaving.

Through the front door, the sound of a neighbor's wind chime, its accidental music, echoes back to us, and the blue clouds in the hills drift farther and farther away. Whatever pain you're having now, whatever pain you would have had turns to rumor, a sunken ship, darkness from which the constellations shine. Hold on tight—I'm carrying you out to the wide streets beneath streetlights and sprawling oaks, and finally out of the valley, onto the empty highway that leads to other cities, other versions of our lives.

Still Life with Unfinished House

We're high up in the rafters of my father's half-built gazebo, close to the tops of the pines, and beyond the pines, the sky breathes in long, blue breaths. My father, my brother, and I are flat on our backs on the unstained wood—its bones exposed. Because he has not yet built the roof, it's only the unstable frame, a clear view to sky, and when the wind gusts up, it sways. We sway—my brother and I on either side of him. I don't think we should be up this high and my head hums with anxiety. I want down, but don't say so because it's my father who's brought us here and he keeps saying we're safe. My brother fidgets, smiles wide, his large brown eyes excited. When he gets too restless, he sits up and my father shushes him down, gently, his hand on my brother's small shoulder or in his thick, gloss-dark hair. "Listen to the wind through the trees," our father tells us. I think of the earth below, swirling with tender ferns, how small I am, how far the fall from here, how my hand throbs in my father's grip. He's stronger than he understands, and I'm caught between enduring his crush and asking him to release me. I stay still, silent. A heavy wind thrills through the branches, and the joints of the gazebo groan. The ladder on which we climbed to this platform scrapes against the wavering structure, and I wonder how we'll get down if the ladder falls. My father closes his eyes. To be good, I also close my eyes, try to imagine my body is weightless. At first, I hover a little over myself, then begin the long drift up. With the sky to my back and my chest full of air, I float up until I can barely see us below in my father's unfinished house. Our faces are too small and obscured by clouds. If we were to fall now, I couldn't save us.

A Momentary Stay against Confusion

I've mentioned before that I used to play piano. I had a small talent—not enough to stay with it or for it to stay with me. Now whenever I find myself (so rarely) in front of one of those grand instruments, there's an ache at my center—just below the heart, just above the stomach—some bright unnamed bird fluttering on a branch in the rain.

In college, before I'd learned how to ward off the falling sense of loneliness, I used to lie awake at night listening to my roommate murmur and gesture in her sleep until I couldn't take it anymore and dressed in the dark, slipped out of the room to the empty halls, echoed down the tile stairs to go outside beneath a shatter of dry stars. It was New Mexico, where everything is dry: my skin, my tongue, the shivering grasses, the Sangre de Cristos looming like great dry ghosts. Even my scuffle across the lot of sleeping cars to the music halls sounded dry to me as it echoed away.

I've never learned to read music, so during the day when the halls were hot and filled with real musicians I stayed away—some unarticulated sense of illiteracy, I suppose. But at night, the halls were empty and I could play alone as loudly, as furiously, as I liked. I made up songs or tried to teach myself little fragments of music I remembered from movies or radio. I knew a few tricks (my hands were small and quick, could add embellishment to melody), but mostly I played bold chords, because they were satisfying and I liked to listen to them reverberate in the small room.

Sometimes I'd go on this way for hours, never beginning or ending a song, but pulling verses, choruses, fragments out of the center of compositions, leading from one fragment into another to build a new song. I liked to stay in the middle of things, so I don't remember when I began to hear the other player in a room down the hall. I must have stopped to shake out my hands or stare out the window when it occurred to me that someone—a real pianist—classically trained in that unfaltering, cascading way, was performing some fantastic piece of music just down the hall. When I began listening it was plaintive and melodic, but soon shifted into sharp, dissonant angles, then slowly, carefully, like the rhetorical modulations of a beautiful speech, it poured into a stately, almost elegiac cadence like summer grass—growing as it withered away.

Then only silence. I listened to the space the music left, waiting for some motion toward another song, but after a while I turned to my own creations to give whomever it was space to contemplate their next articulation. At the end of a particularly long run, I stopped to give my fingers a small rest and was sad to realize the pianist wasn't playing. But then the pianist began a sonata, slow and melancholy like rainclouds. I sat imagining each note falling from the sky into the lifted chest of the piano—glowing there like a new form. I listened all the way through to the nostalgic, trilling end, and finally when the pianist had finished, I turned again to my own simple songs.

This went on for several weeks. Not every night, but many nights I'd let the moon pull me outside and drift across the lot to the piano halls and at some arbitrary point of cessation, I'd realize I heard the pianist in the middle of a song. We never arrived or left at the same time, so I only knew the person by the music—skill and loneliness. Then one night it was particularly late and the pianist had just finished a waltz. After I'd recovered from a strong yawn, I decided it was time to leave and swung the door open and stepped into the hall. Immediately, the door down at the opposite end of the hall swung open and a tall, thin man stepped out. He had large eyes, a shock of white hair, and his skinny arm pointed at me definitively.

"You."

"Yes?"

"You're not a music major." He began walking toward me.

"I'm sorry—do I need some kind of permission?"

"Why aren't you a music major?"

"Because I'm an English major?"

"Well, you're a music major now."

"But, I don't know how—"

"No need to audition for me: you've been doing that for weeks. I'm the department director. You're accepted into the program. Many of those songs are your own, yes? Do you have any formal training?"

"A year of lessons when I was eight."

"Well, you'll train with me."

"I don't know how to read music."

He waved his hands up in the air with a scowl, as if he'd just walked into a swarm of flies.

"That's easy. You can learn that. The other things—the things you already know—can't be taught. I'll teach you the rest."

By now he stood just a few feet away, stiff backed with a kind of midnight intensity shadowing his hollow cheeks. He looked at me with myopic attention. When he noticed my distress, he let the intensity in his face melt into something more amiable, but not quite placid.

"Sorry. I'm not good at introductions. My name is Joe. And your name is . . ."

"Danielle."

"Fine. That's done then. I'll be teaching the music theory class next semester. It's required for all music majors. You should enroll in that and also in individual lessons with me. Come to my office this week so that we can put through the paperwork and set a schedule. You shouldn't waste any more time."

"But I don't know if that's what I want to do."

"Of course it is. Why else would you come here in the middle of the night?"

I don't remember how the conversation ended, only drifting out of the room, back across the lot, and up the stairs, into my dorm room, where I lay there dazed, staring up at the ceiling until I fell asleep.

I did go to his office that week and signed up for the classes he suggested, but insisted that I be a music minor, not a major. He agreed to this, saying that I'd change my mind once I gained some confidence, and in the meantime, I would still be studying music. When I returned from winter break, I went to his office again to agree on a time for our individual lessons.

"I have two times available. One is on Monday. The other is right now." It was Friday on the first week of classes. I was tired of sitting patiently through instructions, and besides, he made me nervous. I felt I needed more mental preparation before I spent an hour at the piano with him.

"Monday."

"I think we should have the lesson now. We need to get started. It's not a real meeting. I just need to know what you can do so I know where we should begin."

"Monday is better for me," I lied. He saw through it, softened his face a little.

"Listen, I know some people find me intimidating, but you really don't have to be nervous. It wouldn't be a real lesson. You would just play something for me and I would listen—just as in the halls."

I insisted again that Monday was better, and he stood back a little, clasped his hands behind his back and nodded.

"Fine, then. Monday it is. I'll see you then."

I tried to smile brightly as I left, to show him he hadn't unnerved me, but of course he had. He gave me a small, concerned smile as I turned away, walked briskly out of the hall—my breath going before me in a white cloud as I left the building. I was relieved to not have to play for him right then, but wondered if I'd hurt his feelings—if it would somehow hinder our new relationship. *I'll see him on Monday*, I thought to myself, *I can worry about it then*. By the time I'd reached the other end of the parking lot, beneath the bare limbs of elms, I was thinking of something else.

We never had the lesson, because Joe died that night.

Perhaps it's cruel for me to tell you this way. Perhaps I should have warned you that this wasn't a story: it happened. In a story, there's shape, there's meaning. A story promises relief—an ordering what can't be ordered. I would like to believe that the stars, the dryness, the description of music, the words with which we speak to one another might mean something more—might finally point to the thing I would never have seen until the moment I see it. But for over a decade I've contemplated this moment of my life—usually on dry, warm nights, when I'm walking alone on a great expanse of pavement beneath the random stars—and after a decade of considering, reading the signs, drawing my mind over these scenes, I've concluded nothing from them.

So, I must conclude that they mean nothing. Perhaps you are disappointed. Perhaps you wanted a more explanatory ending, one that includes the *whole* story. But it's midnight as I write this. The dark outside is the dark of another place, another era of my life, and because my life is not over, part of that past era as well. The small, potted tree I keep by my window is slowly wilting from lack of sunlight. I'm in love, but always anxious. I no longer play the piano. I wish I could give you more, but my life is already moving on, has moved, and I simply drag this story with me. *The whole story*, we like to say, as if the past could be contained.

Acknowledgments

Thank you, first, to Luis Alberto Urrea, whose work I greatly admire, for choosing this manuscript for the AWP Award Series in Creative Nonfiction. Thank you, also, to all those at the Association of Writers and Writing Programs for your hard work and dedication in the promotion of writers and literature.

For their roles in bringing this project to fruition, a special thanks to Regan Huff, Dorine Jennette, and all those at the University of Georgia Press.

I'm grateful to the editors of the following publications, in which some of these essays appeared, sometimes in slightly different versions: *Breach Press*, *Iowa Review*, and *American Literary Review*.

Without the generous guidance and encouragement of Paisley Rekdal, Melanie Rae Thon, Karen Brennan, and François Camoin, and all those in the University of Utah Creative Writing Program, I would not have undertaken this endeavor. I must extend my deep gratitude to six cohorts in particular who read and reread this manuscript at various stages, and whose careful reading made the work better: Rachel Hanson, Susan McCarty, Natanya Ann Pulley, Esther Lee, Nate Liederbach, and Carrie Collier.

Thank you to J. Michael Martinez for fortifying my courage to address the difficult subjects I was, for so long, avoiding. Huge thanks also to two dear friends, Alycia Tessean and Shara Lessley, whose timely insights about this project were invaluable.

For helping me to understand and remember these events more clearly and for their compassion and kindness, I owe a great debt to many people, including Erin Salisbury, Alexis Arczynski, Victoria Fletcher, Aum Kim, Kari Joy, Emma Newman, Vincent Caruso, Josh Hodges, Katie Shultz, Lindsay Bernal, Joellen Pail, Dawn Lonsinger, Shira Dentz, Darci Holtgrave, my sisters, my brother, my mother, and most importantly, Chris Tanseer.